OPEN DOORS

to a

RICHER ENGLISH CURRICULUM

for ages 10 to 13

BOB COX

with Leah Crawford and Verity Jones

Illustrations by Victoria Cox

Crown House Publishing Limited

www.crownhouse.co.uk

First published by

Crown House Publishing Ltd
Crown Buildings, Bancyfelin, Carmarthen, Wales, SA33 5ND, UK
www.crownhouse.co.uk

and

Crown House Publishing Company LLC
PO Box 2223, Williston, VT 05495, USA
www.crownhousepublishing.com

British Library Cataloguing-in-Publication Data
A catalogue entry for this book is available from the British Library.

Print ISBN 978-178583397-7
Mobi ISBN 978-178583450-9
ePub ISBN 978-178583451-6
ePDF ISBN 978-178583452-3

LCCN 2019945823

Printed and bound in the UK by
Gomer Press, Llandysul, Ceredigion

For Lesley, with love

Foreword

I love this book and its companion volume. If I were still a teacher then it would become a key resource for planning, alongside earlier books in the 'Opening Doors' series.

Miroslav Holub's poem 'The Door' has always been one of my favourites (it is included in this volume). I first stumbled across this little gem in an anthology called *Voices*, edited by Geoffrey Summerfield, when I was at school. For me, the poem represented an idea about possibility, having the courage to step through the door, come what may – seize the moment, be brave, be bold and see what happens. It has become a metaphor for my life in many ways. The 'Opening Doors' movement believes that as schools and teachers we should be opening doors of educational opportunity for children by placing great literature at the heart of the English curriculum – and by literature, I mean the whole range of quality writing from poetry to narrative and elegant non-fiction.

Along with Bob Cox, Leah Crawford and Verity Jones, I believe that we should be teaching English as a subject and selecting the texts that we study because of their lasting quality – because they provide challenge, are worth experiencing and broaden a child's reading and writing repertoire. I do not believe that choosing books or poems should be dominated by trying to find a text that matches a topic. That way, English is no longer a subject but the servant of other subjects, on the basis of no solid evidence that the approach improves learning in those subjects, let alone English.

A school that is mapping out an English programme will be thinking about placing the finest literature at the heart of the curriculum. Nothing else will do. The choice of texts needs careful consideration. If children are to enjoy and be able to make something of Walter de la Mare's 'The Listeners' in Year 6, then what progression of texts is needed to provide the stepping stones that gradually and cumulatively prepare children for such richness? How do we build the ability to access challenging literature with confidence so that children can comfortably appreciate, enjoy and, critically, read the very best that literature has to offer? If this is not well considered, and the stepping stones are not carefully mapped, children arrive in Year 6 and are ill-prepared for the demands of poets such Ted Hughes, Edward Thomas, Emily Dickinson, Philip Gross and William Blake.

The 'Opening Doors' movement has been working with great texts and building a repertoire to draw upon when writing with children. The units of work map out possibilities for entering the world of the text, deepening understanding and engagement. The importance of reading aloud should not be underestimated. Children should experience how the language flows, responding to the meaning but also hearing and being moved by the musical tune of the text. It is worth mapping and chorally learning the poems. Key paragraphs or telling sentences could also be learned or performed orally, so that the close and careful study of the texts helps children to internalise the language patterns of great writing. Loitering with great literature, spending time rereading and discussing, and performing with expression allows the language to permeate and embed into children's linguistic competency, adding to their store of imaginative possibility and literary language patterns. Imagine putting the words of William Blake into a child's mind forever!

When Ted Hughes was at Cambridge, he used to get up at five o'clock every morning and read a Shakespeare play. His deep and rich reading put the language and imaginative world of a genius inside his mind. His reading grew his inner world. In the same way, great English teaching grows the imagination and language repertoire of every child through experiencing great literature in depth. If the reading curriculum is meagre, then children will never possess the world of great books and their writing will always be a thin echo of their low-level reading.

'Opening Doors' books are based on what works in classrooms. Over the years, I learned as a teacher that certain texts lend themselves to teaching. For instance, William Blake's 'The Tyger' has always worked well for me in terms of challenging interpretation and leading to deep discussion. Kit Wright's 'The Magic Box' has always stimulated great imaginative writing. Anthony Browne's *Voices in the Park* has never failed to yield up riches during oral comprehension. The units in *Opening Doors to a Richer English Curriculum* have been road-tested and refined in the light of teaching experience. I like the way the authors provide suggestions but expect that the teacher will bring their own ideas to deepen the experience for their children's needs. There is room for performance, drama, taster drafts, mini-writes, imitating lines, writing in response and, of course, deep oral comprehension, where children talk their way to an understanding with the teacher orchestrating the discussion.

Loitering with a worthwhile text that has layers of meaning helps children to move beyond having a passing acquaintance with a poem or story to a deeper relationship. Some children will need to read and reread a text so they can move beyond just being able to decode, shifting into the possibility of deeper understanding. Initial responses can be gathered and discussed, including aspects of what seems significant, interesting or worth discussing, as well as aspects that are mystifying. Spending time discussing vocabulary and the different shades of meaning that so many words and phrases hold is an important part of helping texts to yield up their riches.

What else does an English curriculum need? Across each year, novels, short stories, poetry, non-fiction and film should be identified to build the children's reading and writing stamina. These core books can then be drawn upon during specific units when working with focused texts. A rich reading programme will provide lines of reference and further reading to supplement each unit. Great books will also be useful to develop the children's writing skills: drawing on a range of examples, demonstrating writing techniques such as foreshadowing, and building atmosphere through setting, shift of viewpoint or tension. Such a reading programme provides the daily 'read aloud' sessions for each class and ideally should be supplemented with class sets of books (or at least enough for one between two) so that students can read along, pause, reread and draw upon passages for further work.

Drama can be used to slow the moment in a text, engage emotionally with thought and action, and deepen understanding. Drama also leads well into writing because the writing then arises from the imagined and enacted experience, which throws up more insight and possibility to draw upon when writing. The issue is selecting the right moment and the right activity rather than just deciding to do a bit of 'hot seating'. Where in a text would the reading be deepened through drama, and what strategy should be used? Most teachers have a small repertoire – hot seating, freeze-framing and conscience alley for decision-making – and that's about it! 'Opening Doors' books are full of techniques to extend your toolkit of strategies.

'Opening Doors' approaches also suggest that as teachers we should be writing for and with children to open up possibilities. When shifting into writing, some texts will lend themselves to very obvious imitation. A poem such as 'The Door' could be used as a straightforward model, so the children write an imitation using the same pattern. However, rich reading can also act as a springboard into other ideas and forms of writing. The books list possibilities, but I would also try making a list with the class to open up their ideas and encourage independent thinking.

A key aspect for anyone planning an English curriculum is the notion of developing and revisiting 'key concepts' to create a curriculum that is based on cumulative learning of the big, underlying ideas. This can be supplemented by thinking carefully about deep themes in texts that might be revisited. For instance, the children might experience the story of 'Beauty and the Beast' in Year 2: a tale of a character rejected by society who forms a relationship with someone who sees beyond any physical barrier. This theme may also be revisited in Year 4 through Michael Morpurgo's *Why the Whales Came* or in Year 8 when looking at *The Phantom of the Opera*.

The 'Opening Doors' books leave plenty of space for new texts, enthusiasm and experimentation because the underlying pattern for teaching is easily transferable. The process soon becomes embedded, and that makes teaching easier as our attention shifts from planning the sequence to being able to focus more on the children's learning.

All of this work has to be underpinned by a strong commitment to developing children as readers and writers. In an ideal world, every school would have a wonderfully equipped library so the children have a range of texts to choose from in their individual reading. To acquire fluency and confidence in reading, children may well want to storm their way through popular texts. However, teachers of English will want to grow each child as a reader, introducing them to new authors and styles, nudging them on to richer texts where the reading experience is not just a glib giggle but becomes something deeper and more long-lasting. Children will never really become great readers until they begin to tackle great texts and learn that sustaining their reading with a classic bears fruit. By the same token, they will never become great writers if their reading is thin gruel because their reading will be echoed in their writing.

The 'Opening Doors' teacher is also aware of their own reading and writing life, sharing their love of books with their classes and modelling being a reader. They also enjoy writing for and with their classes, sharing their own drafts as well as composing with the children. In this way, the 'Opening Doors' classroom becomes a community of readers and writers where the challenge of great literature and finely crafted writing, which focuses on the effect on the reader, becomes an everyday joy.

Pie Corbett

Contents

Acknowledgements

The 'Opening Doors' series of books has been developed thanks to feedback and encouragement from schools across the UK (and beyond), and their trialling of materials. It is much appreciated and, indeed, inspiring to hear from so many schools who are using the ideas.

In particular, we would like to thank staff and pupils from:

Alverstoke Junior School, Hampshire
Ash Grove Academy, Cheshire
Aston St Mary's C of E Primary, Hertfordshire
Breamore CE Primary School, Hampshire – with thanks to Emma Clark
The Brent Primary School, London
Briar Hill Primary School, Northamptonshire – with thanks to Ian Hickman
Cherbourg Primary, Hampshire
Chiltern Hills Academy, Buckinghamshire – with thanks to Sue Putnam
Coastlands Primary School, Pembrokeshire – with thanks to Wenda Davies
College Town Primary, Berkshire
Crofton Hammond Infants, Hampshire – with thanks to Jacky Halton
Crookham Junior School, Hampshire
Freegrounds Infants School, Hampshire

Gearies Primary School, Essex – with thanks to Bob Drew
Greenacres Primary Academy, Greater Manchester – with thanks to Tim Roach
Grove Primary School, Redbridge, London
Hale Primary School, Hampshire
Hillcrest Academy, West Yorkshire – with thanks to Sam Collier
Hordle Primary School, Hampshire
Kensington Prep School, Fulham, London
Malmesbury Park School, Dorset – with thanks to Nuala Price
Mottingham Primary School, Bromley, London
Overton Primary School, Hampshire
Poulner Infants School, Hampshire
Poulner Junior School, Hampshire
Red Barn Primary School, Hampshire
Ringwood Junior School, Hampshire
Robin Hood Junior School, Surrey

Rowner Junior School, Hampshire – with thanks to Emily Weaver

Southroyd Primary School, West Yorkshire – with thanks to Emma Kilsby

St Augustine's Catholic Primary School, Surrey

St Lawrence School and Chobham cluster, Surrey

St Mathew's, West Midlands – with thanks to Sonia Thompson

St Oswald's CE Primary School, North Yorkshire

Surbiton High Girls' Preparatory School, Kingston upon Thames, London

Tanglin Trust School, Singapore

Unicorn Trust Schools – with thanks to Sue Robertson

Westbourne Primary School, Surrey

Westbury Park Primary, Bristol

Western Downland Primary School, Hampshire

Wicor Primary School, Hampshire

And also:

Ad Astra Academy Trust

Aspire Education Trust

Centre for Literacy in Primary Education

Hampshire Local Education Authority

Herts for Learning

High Performance Learning – with thanks to Deborah Eyre

Isle of Man, Department of Education and Children

Just Imagine Story Centre

Lancashire Local Education Authority

Leeds Local Education Authority

National Association for the Teaching of English – with thanks to Janet Gough

Optimus Education

Osiris Educational

Research Rich Pedagogies – with thanks to Professor Teresa Cremin and the United Kingdom Literacy Association/ Open University

Talk for Writing – with thanks to Pie Corbett

Write Time – with thanks to Victoria Bluck

Writing for Pleasure – with thanks to Ross Young and Felicity Ferguson

Above all, huge thanks to the team at Crown House Publishing, without whom the 'Opening Doors' series would never have been written!

Introduction

The 'Opening Doors' series has been supporting teachers' passion for quality texts since 2014. At home and abroad, the books have been signposting richer approaches to English in schools keen to exploit the learning opportunities afforded by a depth of challenge for all learners. We have had the pleasure of hearing from many teachers about their pupils' delight in discovering famous writers, their growing relish for learning about a variety of literary styles, and their increasing access to literature and cultural capital. Of course, this applies to all abilities and in some schools this has led to the word 'ability' being reviewed because 'Opening Doors' strategies work on fundamental principles through which *all* learners can be challenged. The highly ambitious approaches offer fresh goals and continual curiosity, but the scaffolds and interventions include and inspire everyone. Each step can represent new knowledge and learning gained in chunks as appropriate for each pupil.

It has been vital that the access strategies enable all pupils to discover just how quirky, fascinating and full of wonder great writing can be. There are big ideas in the extracts and poems we choose for 'Opening Doors', and this is important. The originality and beauty of the text leads the classroom discussion, whilst metaphors, adverbs and prepositional phrases, for example, are taught and modelled in context. Pupils are immersed in reading journeys via quality texts, whilst the dialogic talk, philosophy and teaching of new knowledge combine to create rich learning experiences.

As we have toured schools in the UK and abroad, evidence of the positive impact of challenging texts on pupils' work has grown – there are some examples on the Crown House Publishing website.[1] Have a browse and then make links with the first two books – you could even use the pupils' work as a resource in your lessons.

Teachers learn more themselves every time they explore a challenging new text, and there is a tendency to aim higher as a habit. Once we aspire to something almost out of reach, we might just get there! This goes for teachers and pupils: risk-taking becomes endemic and the acquisition of new vocabulary becomes a daily habit. Some of the new words are only half-grasped initially, but it still represents an important encounter for pupils. Children may have to meet vocabulary in various different contexts over time for the meaning to become fully assimilated. Our own adult relationships with new vocabulary may suggest a similar journey.

In this book, and in its companion for the 6 to 9 age group, we want to show how the use of quality texts is not a separate strand of the curriculum or special content for a project day. It can be an integral part of the whole curriculum, with continuity and progression built in. I (Bob) have been working with co-authors Leah Crawford and Verity Jones on both of these new books, which has been a real privilege. Together, we have provided fifteen units of work (thirty across both volumes) which will give you lots of ideas for building the metalanguage and new knowledge of texts needed to raise standards in the most exciting way possible.

---

1 See https://www.crownhouse.co.uk/featured/opening-doors-to-famous-poetry-and-prose-pupils-work.

Opening Doors to a Richer English Curriculum will support your vision for English, but it will also offer the core principles and detailed units of work that will enable it to be realised. A curriculum with a combination of quality picture books, children's fiction and literature provides a much more appetising diet than is sometimes offered in schools. With effective transition to Key Stage 3, this will become a journey where reading for challenge starts to become the greatest pleasure any child can encounter – nurtured by sensitive and knowing teachers. We have always thought that what teachers do best is to make new learning possible for all. As Timothy Shanahan (2017) observes, 'start kids out with complex texts that they cannot read successfully; then teach them to read those texts well'.

We have included a great range of texts both as the core of each unit and as link reading. We have incorporated some contemporary texts to show how past and present co-exist and how various literary styles can be taught using similar principles, all of which are open to further adaptation. Non-fiction gets a mention too, as many schools have started to apply the key principles for depth to all text types. For the first time, we have also suggested key concepts around which the curriculum can be built, with the units providing examples with which you can work. Developing concepts through which English can be taught will offer you the chance to plan a rich map of learning – one that the whole school will understand. One of the things we have enjoyed most about the 'Opening Doors' series is seeing teachers grow in confidence as the books signpost the way to their own innovations.

We are very much in favour of the 'continuing' part of continuing professional development (CPD), and we want to support teachers' growth and their love of learning. Growing a richer English curriculum will enable the most natural, reflective and evaluative CPD to take place in your classroom every single day. The extra challenges afforded by richer texts will stimulate your own learning far more than standard texts. As teachers, we have to think harder, set more profound questions, play with vocabulary and teach specific concepts – but we get so much more back from our pupils, and there are no dull routines!

Summary of the key principles

As befits a brief introduction, we can only list here the major principles and strategies that have emerged from our work in schools. This is not a model for teaching English, but it is a framework to use as part of your own curriculum design – shaped by you and fit for purpose in your school and with your children. See the framework example on pages 6–7.

Access strategies and 'beyond the limit' link reading

We call this series of books 'Opening Doors' because access is fundamental to new learning. Without the teaching strategies to unlock learning potential, it is likely that new language, genres and styles could be intimidating. But teachers release a whole world of possibility by demonstrating how meaning can be grasped and new literary satisfactions experienced. That's the joy of challenge!

In this book there are a range of access strategies: pictures, questions, links to existing knowledge/experience and slivers of text (adapting the length of the material is far better than excluding anyone from the shared excitement). Each unit has a suggestion for a key strategy with a snappy title. This is designed to support the teaching of comprehension because it enables pupils to start learning about different ways to understand a text.

Of course, it is the link reading that will boost children's comprehension the most. We have worked with schools on linking a range of texts to the core objective and planning for whole-text reading as an expected part of the curriculum. Every term and every year, the objectives and texts get progressively harder, but always within the context of a broad choice. Whereas the term 'wider reading' has often been used, we prefer 'link reading' because it is planned into the curriculum for everyone (see pages 6–7 for an example of the big picture of the objectives and link reading). We also call this the 'beyond the limit' section to emphasise that it is the depth of quality reading expected by schools, linked with reading for pleasure acquired more independently, that will support accelerated progress.

Framework Planning Example

Unit 3: A Fire in My Head

'The Song of Wandering Aengus' by W. B. Yeats

Opening Doors key strategy: symbol source

Objectives which prompt deeper learning journeys:

- ❦ Can you understand how symbols can be used to suggest complex ideas?
- ❦ Can you write an effective poem using symbol and metaphor?

Teach *functional English* as appropriate in this deeper context.

Develop a deeper understanding of symbol source via link reading:

- ❦ 'Woman Skating' by Margaret Atwood
- ❦ 'How to Cut a Pomegranate' by Imtiaz Dharker
- ❦ 'The Door' by Miroslav Holub
- ❦ 'The Call' by Charlotte Mew

Quality text to quality writing journeys:

Apply what you have learnt from W. B. Yeats to write a poem developing your own use of symbol:

- ❦ Seasons
- ❦ Day and night
- ❦ Forests
- ❦ Mountains
- ❦ An oak tree
- ❦ A sapling
- ❦ An item of clothing

In *Understanding Reading Comprehension* (2015: 51), Wayne Tennent argues that 'when children come to the reading of written text they are not blank canvasses. They bring both life and linguistic knowledge to each reading experience.' Schools that are building link reading and simultaneously facilitating reading for pleasure are deepening the knowledge that can be applied to the next challenge.

Taster drafts

The idea of a taster draft is for pupils to write early on in the process to help promote their engagement with, and understanding of, the text. The task is usually time limited and/or word limited. Pupils love the freedom this allows, and teachers love the chance to teach spelling, punctuation and grammar, as well as aspects of style, through the resulting mini-plenaries.

Not only is much of this early learning embedded for the long term, but pupils are also eager to hear the full text. We rarely read out the entire text to the children at the start of the activity, but after attempting their own writing they often beg to hear the famous writer's work. You can hear a pin drop as they listen to the reading. It's no surprise that further questions follow.

Reading journeys

When we mention the word 'comprehension' to pupils in schools, we nearly always get a response which is at best neutral and at worst a shrug or scornful look of boredom. A few times pupils have even said that it is what happens at 2pm every Tuesday! Often there is a link between comprehension and being tested. This doesn't have to be the case. Rather than being something done to you, it can be much more exciting – a reading journey or a dialogue about half-grasped vocabulary or the way a narrative has been expressed. Predictions, questions, new knowledge on technique and effect, and the sharing of ideas can all be part of a reading journey.

You may have your own term, but why not drop the word 'comprehension' if it elicits groans or negativity? In 'Opening Doors' books, we use a big 'Opening Doors' question, with support interventions deployed as appropriate to build skills and knowledge. The glossary also provides prompts for helpful terms and theories. Remember: in your classroom, decisions about the use of resources, questions and strategies pave the way to deeper comprehension for your pupils, so always think of yourself as a pioneer in opening up quality reading routes.

Support questions

Each unit includes an ambitious set of questions, not as a test but to provide a basis for teaching and learning dialogues. The questions are aspirational – a goal for mastery – because all pupils are on a learning journey. Support scaffolds are suggested for those pupils who are struggling, and there are greater depth questions for those who are ready for them. Some pupils will be able to answer the main 'Opening Doors' question without much support, and even move on to the greater depth question if you are happy that their answer is thorough. Advanced pupils should not waste time on anything too easy.

Differentiation occurs through the learning stage, not separate content or objectives.

The radial layouts have proved popular as a tool through which differentiated interventions can be made appropriately for each pupil. Flexibility is vital, so it can be advantageous to create guided groups, according to need, so pupils can learn to the best of their ability at each stage. Some pupils may surprise you in being ready for harder work, whilst other pupils may need more advice and scaffolding. However, greater depth opportunities are always built into expectations.

Excellent responses will (include)

You will find success criteria lists throughout the book, but please don't use them as an arid or discrete list. They are designed to enable teachers to explore just how deep they can go using literary texts. More challenging poems, for example, may need a lot of rereading – but the love of a poem can grow through familiarity. It is possible to prioritise one or two criteria and convert them into child-friendly language. In this way, teaching teams can have rich conversations of their own about language and its effect, about themes and about the appeal of the writing.

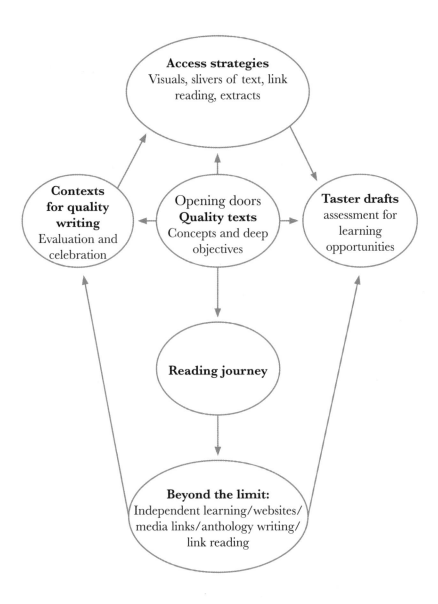

Key concepts

Mapping key concepts at Key Stages 1, 2 and 3 will facilitate a genuine curriculum journey, with revisiting built in via texts which get progressively harder. Remember that you are teaching English, not 'doing' a text. *Opening Doors to a Richer English Curriculum* will signpost your deeper thinking on a map of learning for English. The diagram on page 11 provides a framework for the many ways in which quality writing can be achieved using 'Opening Doors' strategies.

Deep objectives

Having established multilayered concepts for each unit, we have once again suggested using objectives which can go much deeper and through which the concepts can be taught. We have used open-ended questions for these objectives throughout the book because pupils seem to find goals set in question form motivating. Aim to teach aspects of English as part of a richer journey to learning – for example, you can plan for functional English or a targeted aspect of English (like noun phrases) as part of that bigger goal. In this way, spelling, punctuation and grammar can be contextualised much more successfully.

Occasionally, it may be useful to teach pupils about a common misconception. But when lessons focus on one specific aspect of English, especially when this becomes a habit, the curriculum can be narrowed to what we call a 'letter box' approach, with the same few discrete aspects of English delivered and tested. This is the opposite of a curriculum that is deep, rich and full of curiosity.

Wings to fly

Wings to fly are suggested titles with options built in. The phrase actually comes from an evaluation we once heard: that a teacher's pupils had been given 'wings to fly, not drills to kill'. The idea is to learn from a great writer and then apply this creatively to make quality texts link with quality writing.

The 'Opening Doors' team is continually collecting feedback from schools. The acknowledgement list includes just a few of the schools to whom we are grateful for their astute thinking and astonishing work, improving both their pupils' comprehension and writing skills. From this feedback has come a perception that teachers are beginning to use a greater range of literary texts in their curriculum planning, and we certainly hope that we have helped.

I (Bob) call this going 'Beyond the Highwayman', after the famous Alfred Noyes poem which has become a favourite in many primary classrooms. I realised during an INSET I was running that teachers were wary of the difficulties that a new literary text might pose. But when I talked to them about 'The Highwayman', 'The Lady of Shalott' or 'The Listeners' (all poems with challenging and fascinating styles and themes), it emerged that it was more an issue of unfamiliarity when it came to new texts. The complexity of the text was not the problem; there was just the need to get acquainted with it. So, I hope

Opening Doors to a Richer English Curriculum for Ages 6 to 9 will help you all to go 'Beyond the Highwayman'.

Resources

As we have written the series, the following books and organisations have provided particular inspiration and often echoes of the challenge ethos that we all hope to encourage:

Clements, James (2018). *Teaching English by the Book*. Abingdon: Routledge.

Eyre, Deborah (2016). *High Performance Learning: How to Become a World Class School*. Abingdon: Routledge.

Lemov, Doug, Driggs, Colleen and Woolway, Erica (2016). *Reading Reconsidered: A Practical Guide to Rigorous Literacy Instruction*. San Francisco, CA: Jossey-Bass.

Myatt, Mary (2018). *The Curriculum: Gallimaufry to Coherence*. Woodbridge: John Catt Educational.

Roche, Mary (2014). *Developing Children's Critical Thinking Through Picturebooks*. Abingdon: Routledge.

Tennent, Wayne, Reedy, David, Hobsbaum, Angela and Gamble, Nikki (2016). *Guiding Readers – Layers of Meaning: A Handbook for Teaching Reading Comprehension to 7–11 Year Olds*. London: University College London Institute of Education Press.

Centre for Literacy in Primary Education

Just Imagine Story Centre

Let's Think: Cognitive Acceleration

Research Rich Pedagogies – United Kingdom Literacy Association/Open University

Talk for Writing (Pie Corbett)

Part 1

Opening Doors to Poetry

Unit 1

Go and Open the Door

'The Door' by Miroslav Holub

Opening Doors key strategy: shape-shifting

Can you understand some of the ways in which the structure of a poem supports the meaning?

How well can you write your own imaginative poem with a shape and structure which supports your theme?

Access strategies

Miroslav Holub is a famous twentieth-century writer (and immunologist) from the Czech Republic whose poetry has been translated and published across the world. His creative ideas make a big impact on the imagination. Some of his poems, like 'The Door', are very accessible for younger readers. Naturally, the poem made us think about the title of this series, 'Opening Doors'. We always had in mind that it is teachers who welcome new thinking, ideas and opportunities into creative classrooms. The ending of 'The Door' is one of the reasons we chose to start the book with this image: the draught may seem like an anti-climax, but Holub is saying something important. However small the impact, if (metaphorically) the door is opened a fraction, new winds of thinking may blow. Even a draught is a start!

To learn more about structure there are many possible starting points, but why not take a key stanza from the centre of the poem and start to explore vocabulary and potential meaning:

Go and open the door.
   If there's a fog
   it will clear.

Resource 2

Ask the children to note down questions or anything which arouses their curiosity on sticky notes and place them around the text. You could use the illustration here too. Then ask each group to spend two minutes on each of the following questions:

- What did the command and the capital letter 'G' make you think about the style of the poem?
- What associations do you have with fog?
- What associations do you have with doors?
- What associations do you have with doors opening?

This will hopefully produce some surprising comments! A **mini-plenary** now will help you to sift and sort the most original possibilities from the ones making more tenuous links with the imagery.

The discussion that arises during the mini-plenary will give you an opportunity to teach the pupils about imperatives and connotation.

Bob says ...

*In contexts like this, the love of a text grows simultane-
ously with knowledge acquisition. Methodologies can
include a mixture of dialogic talk, direct transmission and
questioning. Step in to introduce or revisit words like ' connotation' when necessary, but always with the understanding
that thoughtful pupil perceptions will make a deeper
impression on their memory.*

A **taster draft** is now possible. Your pupils should write a brief stanza
using a new image – something else beyond the door. You could provide just the opening line:

Go and open the door.

Or, you could offer more scaffolding by including two more lines:

Go and open the door.
   Even if there's only
   the darkness ticking

The stanzas they create should be unusual, perhaps even symbolic,
but they must be coherent. The children are learning how structure
always supports meaning in poetry. Simple **box planning** may help
your pupils if they are stuck: the idea here is to practise the structure
Holub uses by preparing a card for each line.

> Go and open the door.

> Maybe outside there's

> a tree, or a wood,

> a garden,

> or a magic city.

Visualising the structure should help them to understand the importance of layout. The children could imitate Holub's arrangement in their taster draft or adapt it creatively. You could introduce some of the **link reading** at this point, which will help to broaden and deepen their appreciation.

Bob says ...

A focus on a single stanza, or even just a few lines, can support deeper learning. The mind is forced to consider the rationale behind the writer's word choices and layout. Less really can mean more!

These suggestions are very flexible: some pupils may need only the initial line, whilst others may need the full stanza in card form. The

'Opening Doors' strategies are a toolkit of many methodologies to enable teachers to 'feel' for the best learning route appropriate for their pupils. Guided groupings can be useful but these should always be formed according to need. The same thinking applies when the **reading journey** goes deeper after the reading of the full poem.

Your teaching points will depend on the depth of the feedback from the taster draft. Even if your pupils have top-class ideas, there will still be a knowledge gap – in other words, there is always more that you can teach explicitly. Here are some suggestions to explore:

- How have you used capital letters?
- What is the meaning and connotation of the chosen images in your taster draft?
- Did you indent some lines like Holub did? Why?
- How did your layout relate to your meaning?

Bob says …

We have found that excellent progress can be made with quality writing snippets and tasters, which then get developed into sustained writing later on. This type of writing also inspires the children's confidence to engage with harder texts and more unusual styles of writing. We don't just ask pupils to read quality texts to improve quality writing; taster drafts also support the reading progress.

Reading journeys

We always ask the class if they would like to hear the full poem. There is usually an excited cheer because the access strategies have taught them enough to feel confident and to listen well. You could ask them to comment on the ending in particular and to be aware of its importance.

The Door (translated by Ian Milner)

Resource 4

Go and open the door.
    Maybe outside there's
    a tree, or a wood,
    a garden,
    or a magic city.

Go and open the door.
    Maybe a dog's rummaging.
    Maybe you'll see a face,
or an eye,
or the picture
        of a picture.

Go and open the door.
    If there's a fog
    it will clear.

Go and open the door.
   Even if there's only
   the darkness ticking,
   even if there's only
   the hollow wind,
   even if
      nothing
         is there,
go and open the door.

At least
there'll be
a draught.

Throughout 'Opening Doors' there are **radial question** layouts to facilitate your decisions on groupings and support strategies. A central challenging question, often called the 'Opening Doors' question, is set up front and all the pupils are involved in the route to answering it. Each support question is a chunk of knowledge; once mastered well enough it's time to move on. Greater depth challenges are built in, ready for any pupil who has reached the appropriate stage of comprehension.

Bob says ...

The radial questions are an aid to further teaching and learning dialogues. They are not set to be endured as part of a test routine but to be experienced as a fascinating challenge. Comprehension really can be delivered as a reading journey!

As long as progress through the access session has been thorough, the challenging question and support prompts will be attempted by the children with zest. It won't seem intimidating because you have started to model different ways of approaching structure, layout and meaning in bite-size steps. Encourage the pupils to make notes around the text and to regard each support question as a stage towards mastering the 'Opening Doors' question. En route, they should start appreciating the poem deeply and ideas for quality writing will flow with a natural sense of progression. As Michael Rosen says in *What is Poetry?* (2016: 125):

Poems are a midway point between poets and readers. The poet pours in one set of meanings. The reader picks up the poem and puts in another set of meanings, and the two meet somewhere in the middle. That's what reading a poem is all about. It's a conversation between two sets of thoughts: the poet's and the reader's.

There is huge potential in 'The Door' for the kind of 'conversation' that Rosen writes about here. The poem's ambiguity is part of its appeal.

Support:
There are five stanzas. Search for any patterns, repetitions or variations in layout and line length. What might they mean? Explain some examples like 'even if nothing is there'.

Support:
Track the meaning of the images or associations (e.g. 'picture' or 'darkness') stanza by stanza. Use a table if that helps. Show how 'maybe', 'even', 'if' and 'at least' are used to shift our senses.

How does the structure of 'The Door' support the meaning?

Support:
What does the central 'door' image mean to you? Why might 'door' be in lower case? How important is the repetition? Give examples to support your view. What does the ending mean? How would you recite the ending? What is the tone?

Greater depth:
What is your overall interpretation of the meaning of 'The Door'?
Show how punctuation supports the meaning of the poem.
Choose poems from the link reading list and explore how structure supports meaning in different ways.

Excellent responses will:

Key concept: shaping for meaning

❦ Explain how the repetitions, stanza length and line length support meaning.

❦ Explore how images help to create pattern and structure. How does our interpretation grow?

❦ Describe selected examples of shaping for meaning, such as indenting, lines layered for effect (like 'the picture of a picture') and the final shorter stanza.

❦ Show how the punctuation supports shape, structure and meaning.

Key concept: use of symbolism

❦ Discover meaning via association and prior reading: 'magic city', 'hollow wind', 'fog' and 'draught'.

Link your teaching of the **symbolism** and connotations in the poem with other units, like Unit 3 in this book or Unit 15 in *Opening Doors to Quality Writing for Ages 10 to 13*. Unit 1 in *Opening Doors to Famous Poetry and Prose* makes a fascinating link because Charlotte Mew's 'The Call' provides an example of a presence outside a door.

Feed in the link reading suggested on page 27 at any appropriate time. This should not be part of a linear sequence but should deepen understanding for any pupil at any time in the process. Many 'Opening

Doors' schools make the texts available on the tables in front of the pupils and build in silent reading time on a regular basis.

Beyond the limit – link reading

- ❧ 'Fairy Tale', 'Midday' and 'The New House' by Miroslav Holub
- ❧ 'How to Build a Kitchen' by Victoria Adukwei Bulley
- ❧ 'Snow Fox' by Liz Brownlee
- ❧ 'You Are the Ocean' by Abigail Cook
- ❧ 'Childhood' by Frances Cornford
- ❧ 'The Voice' by Thomas Hardy
- ❧ 'The Call' by Charlotte Mew (Unit 1 in *Opening Doors to Famous Poetry and Prose*)
- ❧ 'Ghosts of the London Underground' by Brian Moses
- ❧ 'Underrated' by Karl Nova
- ❧ 'Limited' by Carl Sandburg (available at https://www.bartleby.com/165/35.html)
- ❧ 'Spirit Bridge' by Kate Wakeling
- ❧ 'The Locust Tree in Flower' by William Carlos Williams

Wings to fly

It's now time to develop the taster drafts further or simply apply what has been learnt to a new idea. There will be plenty of scope for originality and choice.

Your pupils might like to bear in mind advice from award-winning poet Kate Wakeling about the writing process: 'I'd say when you begin a poem, first be as wild and messy and free as you can – write as though your pen or keyboard is on fire! – then change hats and become as patient and picky as possible' (quoted in Eagleton, 2019).

The best poems will show that the structure complements the meaning. Use the link reading suggestions to teach the children about variety, past and present. For example, take a look at another award-winning poet's rap collection – Karl Nova's *Rhythm and Poetry* (2017). Encourage your young poets to find a reason for the structures they use to express their ideas. It's also an ideal time to embed what they have learnt about Holub's use of punctuation and to get them reflecting on the purposes of punctuation in a deeper way. They can consciously craft a poem so that every comma is vital to its meaning and interpretation.

Holub's poem has an urgent and commanding voice, which has the purpose of showing, telling and teaching a reader who may never have thought about the theme of opportunity beyond the 'norm'. Ask the children to write a poem guided by one of the following titles and using the same tone – which has a reader in mind who is ready to think and to be inspired!

❦ Go and Open Your Mind …

❦ The Bolted Door

❦ Use inspiration from 'The Door' to write a poem with one of these titles:

   ❧ The Darkness Ticking

   ❧ The Hollow Wind

   ❧ The Picture of a Picture

❦ Write a poem with this line at the start of every stanza except the last one: 'Go and search for a secret'.

❦ Continue 'The Door' from the end of stanza four and add four more stanzas in a similar style. Then end the poem differently.

❦ Develop your taster draft into an original poem.

The ending of 'The Door' lingers long in the mind. It seems like an anti-climax in that the tension rises to a pitch and then flattens, but we think Holub is saying something important: keep even the smallest link open to the imagination, to ideas, to living! Maybe it's relevant that the date of publication is 1962, a few years before the Soviet invasion of Czechoslovakia. The excellent publication *Poems Before and After* (1990) includes a range of poetry which Holub wrote pre- and post-1968.

It matters a lot that we try to develop a personal response from our pupils to poetry. The structures and techniques they learn should be set within the context of a theme that can speak to young and old – like the notion of a door to a deeper life.

If you look now at Unit 4, you can read some pupils' work inspired by 'The Door', where it was used as a link reading text connected with Han-Shan's 'Cold Mountain'.

Unit 2

One Star

'Speak of the North!' by Charlotte Brontë

Opening Doors key strategy: context speaking

How is isolation presented in Charlotte Brontë's poem?

Can you write about silence and being alone in a fresh way?

Access strategies

Charlotte Brontë may be famous for her novels, but readers of 'Opening Doors' have already provided good feedback on her poem 'Mementos' (Unit 9 in *Opening Doors to Quality Writing for Ages 10 to 13*), so we have included her beautiful poem about moors, mountains and loneliness in this volume. It gives you enormous potential to teach about the way a poet creates a 'voice' to express a theme: is this a sad, reflective poem on loneliness or a rumination on the beauty of isolation?

You can start by considering questions the children might explore about the illustration:

❦ What puzzles you?

❧ What might the theme of the poem be?

❧ Which words or phrases could be linked with the scene?

We have seen a lot of exciting thinking and vocabulary development when endings are explored alongside predictions linked with themes. Offer your pupils the last two lines:

And one star, large and soft and lone,

Silently lights the unclouded skies.

We love the use of 'soft' – it deserves some discussion. Use a diagram like the one below – perhaps call it a **context search** – and ask the children for as many uses of the word 'soft' as possible by using it in a sentence.

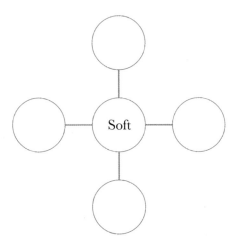

The need to understand new vocabulary is critical, but the need to contextualise it is equally important. That's why we have called the key strategy here 'context speaking'. This will emerge from years of reading, discussing and even (we hope) falling in love with words: 'Most vocabulary growth results incidentally from massive immersion in the world of language and knowledge ... It has long been known that the growth of word knowledge is slow and incremental, requiring multiple exposures to words' (Hirsch Jr, 2003; quoted in Bleiman, 2018).

The feedback you get from your pupils should illustrate that simple words can be used in many ways in literature and in life. When we think about the star in 'Speak of the North!' it is fairly easy to grasp 'large' and 'lone', but the suggestion that it is 'soft' takes the reader further.

- ❦ Does soft have a gentle association?
- ❦ Is the star at ease, figuratively?
- ❦ Does this help us to understand a more positive image of loneliness?

Teachers can take their pupils further using these kinds of questions. Independent reading for pleasure is vital, of course, but in the limited number of hours when pupils have the advantage of your skill and knowledge, this kind of experience counts for much.

Bob says ...

Plan for quality reading and enrichment in the precious hours you have teaching your pupils. The children will discover authors, books and poems they could not find without you. That's life enhancing!

Now apply your pupils' thinking about the potential ambiguity of simple words in an imaginative context by asking for a **taster draft**. Working in pairs, one pupil should write the first two lines of a poem about isolation and the other pupil should write the last two lines – and then match them up like bookends! They can have fun questioning each other's thinking: who has used a simple word, perhaps an adjective, in a clever way?

In whole-class feedback, tease out the most promising word usage ready for more sustained writing later on.

Reading journeys

Speak of the North!

Resource 7

Speak of the North! A lonely moor
Silent and dark and tractless swells,
The waves of some wild streamlet pour
Hurriedly through its ferny dells.

Profoundly still the twilight air,

Lifeless the landscape; so we deem,
Till like a phantom gliding near
A stag bends down to drink the stream.

And far away a mountain zone,
A cold, white waste of snow-drifts lies,
And one star, large and soft and lone,
Silently lights the unclouded skies.

The taster draft should already have prompted some **writing for reading** links. You can now distribute the support questions as appropriate, so all your learners can progress together towards answering the central, challenging question. See figure on page 36.

Excellent responses will:

Key concept: meaning in context

- 🍃 Explain links across the images of moor, stream, mountain and star.

- 🍃 Explore how the poet conveys meaning.

- 🍃 Include some effective examples of ways in which isolation is expressed, like the stag appearing and being likened to a 'phantom'.

- 🍃 Show that the meaning of the words has been comprehended in context. Are the mountains a 'waste' or are the snow-drifts a wild thing of beauty?

Support:

In a table, list the words associated in the poem with moor, stream, mountain and star. What links are there?

Support:

Which figures of speech contribute to the 'lonely' images? Search for a simile, personification or metaphor.

How is loneliness portrayed by Charlotte Brontë?

Support:

Why does the poem begin with an exclamation about the North?

Greater depth:

Make your case for the extent to which the poet's images of the moor encourage thoughts either of isolation or a beauty in loneliness. Incorporate all you have learnt.

Compare these images with others in your link reading.

As in all 'Opening Doors' books, the purpose of the excellence criteria is to guide discussion about new texts within teaching teams. It is not intended to be a tick-list for pupils.

Bob says …

The important principle is that you become aware of the potential depth available within a text to transmit the key concepts to pupils. It may take a number of times of teaching this unit but your confidence will build. Then the success criteria can start to link into the questions you ask and support the content you are delivering.

Beyond the limit – link reading

You could set aside curriculum time for your pupils to start on all sorts of **link reading** which will deepen the context for Charlotte Brontë's poem. The following suggestions all contain fascinating uses of vocabulary, with even simple words taking on fresh imaginative life. These texts cover a huge range of styles, past and present, to help pupils learn about vocabulary used in many different ways.

- ❦ 'Lines Composed in a Wood on a Windy Day' by Anne Brontë
- ❦ 'Mementos' by Charlotte Brontë (Unit 9 in *Opening Doors to Quality Writing for Ages 10 to 13*)
- ❦ 'By St Thomas Water' by Charles Causley
- ❦ 'The Alphabest' by Carol Ann Duffy
- ❦ 'Cold Mountain' by Han-Shan (see Unit 4)

- ❦ 'The Way Through the Woods' by Rudyard Kipling
- ❦ 'A Star Here and a Star There' by Alice Oswald
- ❦ 'Lyrical Exercises' by Karl Nova
- ❦ 'The Snitterjipe' by James Reeves
- ❦ 'Night Skating' by Vernon Scannell
- ❦ 'Escape at Bedtime' by Robert Louis Stevenson
- ❦ *Dark Sky Park: Poems from the Edge of Nature* by Philip Gross
- ❦ *The Hound of the Baskervilles* by Sir Arthur Conan Doyle (Unit 6 in *Opening Doors to Quality Writing for Ages 10 to 13*)

Wings to fly

Try to link the quality text **reading journey** with quality writing opportunities. Maintain the theme of vocabulary in context and with distinctive meaning, continuing to emphasise how great writers become very dextrous at using ordinary words for original purposes.

It's now time to imitate! Your pupils can practise and improve their skills as wordsmiths by writing their own poem. Here are some suggestions with links to Charlotte Brontë's poem:

- ❦ Write about a 'soft' moon.
- ❦ 'A cold white waste of snow-drifts lies'. Continue …
- ❦ The Lonely City
- ❦ Home Alone
- ❦ Speak of the North! (or Speak of the South/East/West)

❦ A Lonely Photograph

❦ A Journey Alone: Fears and Fascination

❦ Star!

The Brontë sisters grew up in a parsonage in Haworth, from where they used to walk to a waterfall (now called the Brontë Waterfall) on the moors above the village. It's a spot visited by tourists from all over the world. Why not take your pupils on a visit to the Brontë Parsonage Museum and for a walk across the moors? This will bring them close to both the wonder and the isolation of the moors. I (Bob) can remember taking some fantastic teenagers there over twenty years ago. That was when the Brontës' poetry and, of course, the memorable scenes from their novels, took on a deeper meaning for the students: it matched the setting with the words. Learning outside the classroom can be as important in English as in any other subject when building a richer curriculum for all.

A Fire in My Head

'The Song of Wandering Aengus' by W. B. Yeats

Opening Doors key strategy: symbol source

Can you understand how symbols can be used to suggest complex ideas?

Can you write an effective poem using symbol and metaphor?

Access strategies

'The Song of Wandering Aengus' is a popular poem by William Butler Yeats written in 1899. Aengus is the god of love, youth and beauty in Irish folklore, but the theme of the 'fire in the head' can be appreciated in the context of any kind of passion. You can teach your pupils much about the use of motif, symbol and metaphor by exploring the images and path of the events in the poem.

Build towards a full reading by starting with the key lines:

I went out to the hazel wood,
Because a fire was in my head,

Resource 9

Collect the children's ideas on the potential meaning of a 'fire in the head' – beyond the literal! What might fire represent?

Next, ask them to list five ways in which the image of fire might be used in the rest of the stanza. Prompts for those who are stuck could include:

❧ Is the fire going to be exciting or painful?

❧ Is the fire psychological?

❧ How will the hazel wood setting be developed?

Now introduce the illustration to deepen the enquiry:

❧ What might happen next?

❧ What do you notice in the bubble which makes up most of the drawing?

❧ What kind of concept might be imagined in a bubble?

Reading journeys

You can now ask the children to read the first two stanzas of the poem:

Resource 10

I went out to the hazel wood,
Because a fire was in my head,
And cut and peeled a hazel wand,
And hooked a berry to a thread;
And when white moths were on the wing,
And moth-like stars were flickering out,
I dropped the berry in a stream
And caught a little silver trout.

When I had laid it on the floor
I went to blow the fire aflame,
But something rustled on the floor,
And someone called me by my name:
It had become a glimmering girl
With apple blossom in her hair
Who called me by my name and ran
And faded through the brightening air.

Apply a **symbol source** analysis to these stanzas. This will focus the children's minds on the overall meaning and encourage interpretations of the vocabulary, not just literal meaning. This is a vital **reading journey** for your pupils as they will learn how to access both literal and figurative language. Those who are best at it are likely to be pupils with a wider reading world and background, which is why so many educationalists advise that children read a broad range of texts both at school and at home. Symbol source is a way of making the teaching of symbols in literature more explicit and therefore more transferrable. Encourage your pupils to evaluate the use of symbols in any new texts they encounter, but always in the context of the overall meaning.

Use the following table to explore any associations the children may have with specific words or phrases: the symbol source that will start to unlock meaning. See how many associations they can build independently. Then, use a **mini-plenary** to sift and sort their suggestions and teach directly about any connotations which have not been so deeply appreciated. Using the 'beyond the limit' texts at this point may also help the discussion. Encourage note-taking and curiosity right through the exercise. Words are fascinating and mysterious, especially in texts which challenge the mind. We've included some examples to kick-start the process.

Word/phrase	Association
hazel wand	Stick Rural setting Wand sounds like magic too

Word/phrase	Association
moth-like stars	Night Are the stars flapping like moths?
apple blossom	Spring, new life, youth How does this link with the girl?

We're picturing your classroom with lots of excited hands up and lots of fascinating ideas about words and images being offered. Symbol source work can stimulate the exploration of images with wider representative meaning across many poems. Irish folklore provides the backdrop to Yeats' poem, but many mythologies include fantasy visions of youth and pastoral delight. Shakespeare calls on this tradition in *A Midsummer Night's Dream* when Bottom expects an idyll in the woods and ends up turned into an ass!

Bob says ...

Use a dialogic approach with this table. It involves a combination of learning, questioning and teacher intervention. You are helping the children to fall in love with the poem and understand it.

You can explore **dialogic talk** further by browsing the Let's Think in English website: www.letsthinkinenglish.org. Let's Think principles are drawn from research by Jean Piaget and Lev Vygotsky that young people learn best when exploring ideas together. Leah Crawford, a Let's Think consultant and co-author of 'Opening Doors', says: 'We make progress when we are challenged at the upper limit of our thinking.'

Before reading the full poem, give the pupils the first lines of the third stanza:

Though I am old with wandering
Through hollow lands and hilly lands,
I will find …

Resource II

Now, ask the children for a **taster draft** – to complete stanza three with five more lines. Your pupils need to imitate Yeats by developing the same images and symbols. Look carefully at the rhyme scheme – there are some interesting repetitions from which your budding poets might learn. In your assessment of their work, try to refine their symbolism and, of course, celebrate the best examples. What they learn from Yeats – and from you – they can deepen in the **wings to fly** section.

Here are some excellent examples of taster drafts from pupils at Coastlands Primary School in Pembrokeshire:

I will find what lies beyond,

And hold my lover in my hands,

Those hands that once could hold her close

And dance and sing across the wood.

But when she turned to scales once more,

To go with her, I wish I could.

Olivia Beal and Sophie Marshall

I will find that obscure maiden fair,

I long to hold her in my hands;

And seek I shall till end of days

And travel by sea and search on shore –

Her face so stunning in my mind –

To be with her forever more.

Caitlyn Hawkins and Madeleine Beal

You might wish to use this reading of the full poem by Michael Gambon: https://www.youtube.com/watch?v=cN_VPtGfsw0.

The Song of Wandering Aengus

Resource 12

I went out to the hazel wood,
Because a fire was in my head,
And cut and peeled a hazel wand,
And hooked a berry to a thread;
And when white moths were on the wing,
And moth-like stars were flickering out,
I dropped the berry in a stream
And caught a little silver trout.

When I had laid it on the floor
I went to blow the fire aflame,
But something rustled on the floor,
And someone called me by my name:
It had become a glimmering girl
With apple blossom in her hair
Who called me by my name and ran
And faded through the brightening air.

Though I am old with wandering
Through hollow lands and hilly lands,
I will find out where she has gone,
And kiss her lips and take her hands;
And walk among long dappled grass,
And pluck till time and times are done,

The silver apples of the moon,
The golden apples of the sun.

Assess which pupils are ready for a harder question to test progress with overall understanding:

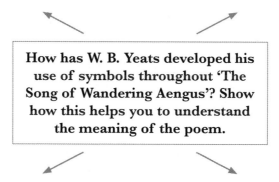

> **How has W. B. Yeats developed his use of symbols throughout 'The Song of Wandering Aengus'? Show how this helps you to understand the meaning of the poem.**

The children can apply all they have learnt to this challenge, with support given as appropriate:

- ❦ Evidencing ideas from the text.

- ❦ Trialling an example in a single paragraph first (e.g. the symbol of the apple).

- ❦ Modelling the development of a symbol (e.g. images of the countryside) with reference to the link reading and other instances you can find. Exploring with the children how some examples, however brief, are original and interesting will introduce **intertextuality** and cross-referencing.

❦ Developing the word/phrase association table (on pages 44–45) to evaluate associations in the poem.

❦ Sticky notes and questions placed around the full text on a sheet of A3 paper.

Greater depth tasks might include:

❦ Why is the poem called a 'song'?

❦ Explain the rising tone of the third stanza: what do you think the ending implies?

❦ From the time of the Ancient Greeks, poets have adapted the tradition of the rural idyll which is connected with love, beauty and country life. Find out more about the pastoral tradition in poetry. Try this link to get started: https://www.poets.org/poetsorg/text/pastoral-poetic-term.

❦ Read 'Elegy Written in a Country Churchyard' by Thomas Gray.

Whatever method you use, layer in the support when needed and choose guided groups according to the progress being made on this **deep objective**. All learners can participate in 'Opening Doors' challenges.

Yeats' famous poem is multilayered. Meaning can work in our minds in a basic way – for example, we can identify the linear order of events, such as Aengus going fishing. But a lifetime passes following the flight of the glimmering girl and his continuing quest to rediscover her; the complexity and the curiosity grow simultaneously. We can then use symbol sourcing to discover deeper implications through the use of fire, apples and quests.

Advanced readers may also like to speculate on the poem being about lost love or life – long-held passions of any kind where even old age brings new hopes. The access strategies should ensure that the children have an emotional response to the work, alongside a growing fascination with the sound, overall meaning and ancient mystery of the poem. Then the 'Opening Doors' question will start to unlock the knowledge needed to relate the symbols to the unfolding philosophy.

Bob says …

If the emotional response, supported by access tools, comes first, then learning about the techniques can deepen the love of a poem.

Excellent responses to the 'Opening Doors' question on page 49 will:

Key concept: symbol

❦ Explain, with examples, how the symbols in the poem deepen meaning and appreciation.

❦ Offer links between some symbols and the pastoral tradition.

❦ Interpret the poem in the light of the main symbols.

In *How Texts Teach What Readers Learn*, Margaret Meek (1988: 38) writes about the many ways in which young readers grasp textual ambiguities: 'One of the sharpest late reading lessons I have learned is to *let* the texts teach the reader.' With the right kind of interactions, your pupils should be discovering new meaning in this poem beyond the original objectives because the quality of the writing is so high.

Lily Courie, another Coastlands Primary School pupil, responded with great depth to this famous poem:

How has W. B. Yeats developed his use of symbols throughout 'The Song of Wandering Aengus'? Show how this helps you to understand the meaning of the poem.

In 'The Song of Wandering Aengus', the most used symbol that permeates the whole poem is 'light'. The poem begins with the speaker, Aengus, going out into the wood because 'a fire was in my head'. Aengus was the God of Love and Beauty in Celtic mythology. The 'fire' is maybe a feeling of deep love or passion for the 'glimmering girl' (another image using light) that is referred to in stanza two.

The first and second stanzas seem to take place at dawn, when 'moth-like stars were flickering out'. Aengus 'went to blow the fire aflame' and the 'glimmering girl' appears but then 'fades through the brightening air'. Perhaps the girl is in his imagination and fades when he realises she was only in his head?

Also in the poem, other symbols are used associated with the maiden, like: apple blossom, sun and hazel. The apple blossom might symbolise spring, life, beauty or youth. The hazel wand reminds us of magic because witches and other magic beings usually have wands.

We love the way that Lily has developed such a clear expression of how she understands the symbolism without ever losing her personal response to the poem.

Beyond the limit – link reading

The following poems all make interesting use of symbols and will provide excellent cross-references to 'The Song of Wandering Aengus':

❧ 'Woman Skating' by Margaret Atwood

❧ 'How to Cut a Pomegranate' by Imtiaz Dharker

❧ 'Fairy Tale' by Miroslav Holub

❧ 'The Door' by Miroslav Holub (Unit 1)

❧ 'Being Old' and 'I Dream a World' by Langston Hughes

❧ 'The Thought Fox' by Ted Hughes

❧ 'Prince Kano' by Edward Lowbury (Unit 6 in *Opening Doors to a Richer English Curriculum for Ages 6 to 9*)

❧ 'The Call' by Charlotte Mew (Unit 1 of *Opening Doors to Famous Poetry and Prose*)

❧ 'Fern Hill' by Dylan Thomas

Wings to fly

It's now time to apply what was learnt from the predictive stanza to a poem that uses symbols to represent wider ideas or possibilities. Rather than suggest titles, it might be better to give your pupils a free choice – the **link reading** will have helped. Structure will assist any pupils who are struggling, so you could suggest some symbols which might already have imaginative associations – for example:

- Seasons
- Day and night
- Forests
- Mountains
- An oak tree
- A sapling
- An item of clothing

A writing tip might be to encourage the exploration of one symbol first to avoid a jumble of descriptions. It's easy to try too hard! Some pupils will respond well to being given three stanzas, like the Yeats poem, to develop and complete a story that incorporates symbols.

Bob says ...

Learning about symbols should release creativity rather than inhibit flow, so the biggest challenge here is maintaining the children's pleasure in their work and ensuring their writing has a natural rhythm. Emphasise that excellent responses will display coherence, leaving the reader to reflect on the ending. This unit provides good practice in writing deliberately with ambiguity in mind.

Here is a poem by a Year 6 pupil from Coastlands Primary School once more. The reading link provided the inspiration, especially the Ted Hughes poem.

The ticking of a clock echoes in my mind,
Empty. Nothingness. An enormous crater.
Tick! Everything is shrouded in darkness.
But in the wasteland, a light flickers and grows.

Trees sprout, grass emerges,
Tendrils creep, reach for the sun.
Fronds unfurling endlessly,
Fruitful hedges blossoming.

Empty at first, icy droplets emerge.
Slowly the void fills,
Drop by drop.
Streams trickle, rivers run.

Until finally the crater is a lake,
Glistening, thriving with life.
Critters crawl, creatures creep,
The idea is fully formed.

Madeleine Beal

Unit 4

Among the White Clouds

'Cold Mountain' by Han-Shan

Opening Doors key strategy: extended metaphor

Can you build your understanding of an extended metaphor in poetry?

Can you write an original poem with your own metaphor extended effectively?

Han-Shan was supposedly a ninth-century poet who is associated with the Chinese Tang Dynasty. He seems to have led his life in simplicity and seclusion, even writing some of his poems on rocks. Thanks to dedicated translators, we can enjoy the beauty of Han-Shan's words today. In this unit we will look at some short sections from his 'Cold Mountain' poems, which will provide a marvellous resource for your pupils to appreciate how the mountain metaphor is extended and how the wonder of poetry has deep and global roots.

Access strategies

Once your pupils start to engage with the cold mountain image, they will start thinking of all the places they have visited which seemed both beautiful and threatening. We would suggest using the first two lines from three selected stanzas, as presented below, to begin learning about the extension of a metaphor:

Men ask the way to Cold Mountain
Cold Mountain: there's no through trail.

I settled at Cold Mountain long ago,
Already it seems like years and years.

Clambering up the Cold Mountain path,
The Cold Mountain trail goes on and on:

Use a **mind link strategy** to explore exactly what each of the couplets might mean in a metaphorical way:

Stanza 1: Men ask the way ...	What do 'cold' images mean? Is it literal or does it have a wider meaning?	Why do people 'ask the way'?	What does a 'through trail' mean?

Stanza 2: I settled ...	What exactly does 'settled' mean?	Has 'long ago' got an exact time context?	Why is 'years' repeated?
Stanza 3: Clambering up ...	Define 'clambering'.	What image does 'trail' have for you?	How does 'on and on' link with 'years and years'?

This analysis will lead to very rich **dialogic talk** if you ask different groups to address different couplets and feed back their ideas to the class. Emphasise how much poetry relies on our experience of vocabulary and meaning for interpretation. Improving comprehension is as much about our life experiences and the words we have read as about any class strategy.

It will be fascinating now to ask your pupils to draft the content of each stanza, though not necessarily as a poem at this stage. The idea is for them to understand that 'cold mountain' is a metaphor and how fresh concepts can extend the initial idea. Ideally, they will begin to use metaphor to link their three stanzas together. Visuals and illustrations may well support their thinking as they build their own meaning from the 'cold mountain' image.

These **taster drafts** should enable the children to experiment and ask further questions. How well can they capture the essence of the 'cold mountain'? Use assessment for learning at its most powerful to refine and improve their image-making. A cold mountain could be a stark but beautiful place which is only accessible on foot, and perhaps dangerous too, but it could also be sacred or spiritual. What does the phrase mean to you and your pupils?

I (Bob) first came across the 'Cold Mountain' poems in *Rose, Where Did You Get That Red?* by Kenneth Koch (1973). It is a superb book in which Koch outlines his own teaching journey. He observes: 'My poetry ideas were good ideas as long as they helped the children make discoveries and express feelings, which is what made them happy about writing' (Koch, 1973: 111). He also makes the link between quality texts and quality writing, which of course plays an integral role in enhancing young learners' engagement with literature.

The following taster draft by Sara Elkhoulfi from Greenacres Primary Academy was inspired by Han-Shan:

The beautiful scenery was a palette of winter and spring.

The mountain range was a skate-park with snowy ramps.

The range of mountains was a frozen city.

This was edited and improved following feedback from her inspiring teacher, Tim Roach:

The allure of the scenery was a palette of winter and spring.

The steaming waterfall was cascading over the Cold Mountain.

The frothy milk was hiding the mountains.

Reading journeys

Your pupils will now enjoy comparing their own drafts with these stanzas from Han-Shan.

Resource 15

6.

Men ask the way to Cold Mountain
Cold Mountain: there's no through trail.
In summer, ice doesn't melt
The rising sun blurs in swirling fog.
How did I make it?
My heart's not the same as yours.
If your heart was like mine
You'd get it and be right here.

7.

I settled at Cold Mountain long ago,
Already it seems like years and years.
Freely drifting, I prowl the woods and streams
And linger watching things themselves.
Men don't get this far into the mountains,
White clouds gather and billow.
Thin grass does for a mattress,
The blue sky makes a good quilt.

Happy with a stone underhead
Let heaven and earth go about their changes.

8.
Clambering up the Cold Mountain path,
The Cold Mountain trail goes on and on:
The long gorge choked with scree and boulders,
The wide creek, the mist-blurred grass.
The moss is slippery, though there's been no rain
The pine sings, but there's no wind.
Who can leap the world's ties
And sit with me among the white clouds?

Choose appropriate **reading journeys** from the **radial questions** on page 63. Remember to engage with your pupils when gauging their level of difficulty.

Excellent responses will:

Key concept: extended metaphors

- ❦ Show understanding of how the images reflect a journey and explain this with reference to the text.

- ❦ Explore some detailed examples of the way the descriptions reflect harshness yet fulfilment.

- ❦ Demonstrate how an **extended metaphor** can lead the reader in their own interpretations.

Support:
Mark the language which suggests the difficulties of making it to the top of Cold Mountain.

Support:
Focus on images of nature: what do they tell us?

Support:
Explain: 'The blue sky makes a good quilt', 'choked' and 'Who can leap the world's ties'.

How does Han-Shan describe Cold Mountain?

Support:
Can you track Han-Shan's feelings through the poem?

Greater depth:
Can you interpret the metaphor of 'cold mountain' by referring to the text? What does it mean to you?

Hints: discovery, meditation, struggles.

The stanzas from Han-Shan have huge potential for dialogic talk, as well as **didactic teaching**, to introduce extended imagery in poetry. 'Opening Doors' questions are often set out in a radial way to give maximum flexibility and to encourage depth for all learners, rather than discrete pathways for set 'abilities'. The questions work best when learning dialogues, talking partners and teacher explanations go hand in hand.

Bob says ...

It's the beauty of the writing that leads to a greater appreciation of the content. Pedagogy should be a tool to understand more about how pupils can access that beauty. Recommended pedagogies tend to change over time; the central impact of the text remains.

Beyond the limit – link reading

Many thematic links are possible, but we've chosen poems which extend ideas with a wide metaphorical application.

- ❦ 'The Fish' by Elizabeth Bishop
- ❦ 'Eden Rock' by Charles Causley
- ❦ 'The Snowflake' by Walter de la Mare
- ❦ 'Valentine' by Carol Ann Duffy
- ❦ 'Stopping by Woods on a Snowy Evening' by Robert Frost
- ❦ 'The Door' by Miroslav Holub (Unit 1)
- ❦ 'Mother to Son' by Langston Hughes

❦ 'The Path' by Edward Thomas (Unit 5 in *Opening Doors to Famous Poetry and Prose*)

❦ 'Fern Hill' by Dylan Thomas

Pupils from Greenacres Primary Academy used the **link reading** (specifically 'The Door') to inspire these drafts:

As the hinges creaked open, a handful of dust flew in through the gap, which made me sneeze. A shining light blasted in, nearly making me blind. The door opened, a group of finger-pricking cacti could be seen in the distance.

In the foreground, I could see an arid desert. It was as dry as a pineapple, not cut or washed. Crabs' and scorpions' clicking claws could be heard. I could taste the fresh smell of dates hanging on palm trees.

I stepped out and the feet-burning sand burnt my feet. Looking closer, I saw old and enchanted bones laying on the sand. Huge temples stood with doors to enter.

Mehak Tahir

As the door loudly creaked open, a refreshing breeze came drifting through the entrance, carrying its fragrance with it. The smell filled the room with the scent it was holding.

In the foreground were fire ants, chimpanzees and pythons, roaming around the place. Gathering around the place were bamboo sticks. The spreading roots of the palm trees all around the tree. In the distance, there were faint noises such as birds tweeting, snakes hissing, twigs snapping, fire cracking and lions roaring. There was a rock formation and inside were idols and a lost temple. Then, I knew they were ancient and from China or Italy. The rainforest was littered with a century of detritus: rubbish, moss, bark and leaves. I was a bit scared, so I walked across. Then, I saw the waterfall.

Mumina Hussain

Wings to fly

One option for sustained writing is to develop the taster draft ideas into metaphorical images inspired by the 'Cold Mountain' title itself. This could mean poems crafted around, for example:

❦ The mountain as a journey to be undertaken.

❦ The mountain as a spiritual retreat.

❦ The mountain as a harsh place of struggle.

❦ The mountain as a healthy challenge.

Another option is to apply what has been learnt from Han-Shan to new themes which have the potential for the children to practise the extended metaphor concept. Here are some possibilities:

❦ A rose

❦ A river

❦ A briar

- ❦ A mobile phone
- ❦ Books
- ❦ An onion
- ❦ A crown
- ❦ A bridge

Those pupils who excel can create lots of drafts or poems for their anthologies. If the option of an anthology is planned for regularly in your curriculum design, then pupils will get to experience much more poetry reading and writing across the school. The link reading will also help to immerse them in many different literary texts based around the key concept. For example, in this unit, if the children craft poems using a number of different metaphors, they are practising and improving in ever broader and deeper ways. There is also a huge personal investment in an anthology which many pupils enjoy.

You could use these questions to prompt expectations:

- ❦ What other kinds of feelings can be expressed via different metaphors?
- ❦ Can you extend the metaphor stage by stage, unravelling more meaning and taking unexpected turns en route?

In the 'Cold Mountain' poems, Han-Shan reflects on the feelings of calmness and strength that come from reaching a place to which there is no path. It could be that your pupils may, metaphorically, take a similar cognitive journey where unusual challenges and uncertain routes ahead may offer a greater fulfilment in the end.

Unit 5

The Bird That Sings

'Sympathy' by Paul Laurence Dunbar

Opening Doors key strategy: the power of contrast

Can you understand how injustice can be expressed through contrast?

Can you use contrast to express injustice with poignancy?

This unit introduces readers to Paul Laurence Dunbar, a journalist, essayist, storywriter and poet who was writing towards the end of the nineteenth century in Dayton, Ohio. Dunbar was one of the first influential African-American writers. As the son of freed slaves, his route to gaining recognition as an author was fraught with condescension and prejudice. Rather than studying law, as was his desire, he began life as an elevator operator, due to his mother's limited finances and the colour of his skin.

Much is left unsaid in his poem 'Sympathy'. Its **extended metaphor** expresses the specific continuing agony of 'freed' African-Americans and, more broadly, the agonies of all those who are trapped by inequality and discrimination.

Access strategies

Read the following excerpt from the first stanza of the poem. Explain to the children that the lines depict a sensory scene. As they listen, can they picture the scene and try to sense the mood?

When the sun is bright on the upland slopes;

When the wind stirs soft through the springing grass,

And the river flows like a stream of glass;

When the first bird sings and the first bud opes,

And the faint perfume from its chalice steals –

You may need to clarify the meaning of words such as 'upland' (high ground) and 'chalice' (a goblet, often given as a trophy). The other visual images are quite simple, but the mood is strong.

Ask your pupils to choose a line they like and share with a partner why they like it. How does the line make them feel? What do they notice about its sound when it is read aloud? The pairs could snowball to fours and speak their lines aloud and share their thoughts, before going deeper with the following question:

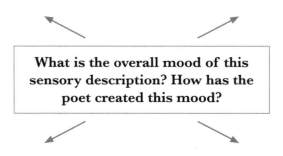

What is the overall mood of this sensory description? How has the poet created this mood?

The pupils may draw attention to:

- 🐦 The choice of adjectives: 'bright', 'soft', 'springing', 'first', 'faint'. There is a mood of gentle warmth and new life.

- 🐦 This is mirrored in the verb choices: 'stirs', 'flows', 'sings', 'steals', 'opes' (an archaic form of opens), which suggest gentle but constant free movement.

- 🐦 The variety of senses attended to: sight, touch, smell and sound.

- 🐦 The repetition of 'first' emphasises new life.

- 🐦 The repeated sounds are sibilant – the soft 's' and 'w' add to the mood.

- 🐦 There is a central simile which offers a moving visual.

- 🐦 Nouns like 'glass', 'chalice' and 'perfume' refer to a world of rich and precious materials, even though this is a natural outdoor landscape.

If there are aspects of the poem the pupils haven't noticed, don't be afraid to mention them directly, but relate them to the mood the children have already begun to build for themselves.

Leah says ...

What is most important – and this is an aspect of teaching literature that we are in danger of losing – is that your pupils make connections with the text in order to build meaning. What does it invite them to see and feel? The power of this poem hinges on the reader sensing a contrast in mood, not in spotting poetic techniques. Make connections and personal responses before exploring how the writer has elicited these responses.

Once the children are sounding secure in their understanding of mood, it's time to show them the complete stanza:

I know what the caged bird feels, alas!
    When the sun is bright on the upland slopes;
When the wind stirs soft through the springing grass,
And the river flows like a stream of glass;
    When the first bird sings and the first bud opes,
And the faint perfume from its chalice steals –
I know what the caged bird feels!

Resource 18

How has the mood and the message of the first stanza changed with the added refrain? Why might the poet know how the caged bird feels?

The power of contrast for a writer lies in not having to explain your message, but rather inviting your reader to feel it. The juxtaposition of free, gentle growth and movement with the image of the caged bird enables the poet to speak the unspeakable.

You may wish to draw attention to the rhythm if you feel that your class are ready. An **iambic rhythm** (de-dum de-dum de-dum de-dum de-dum) is the 'base' rhythm of lyric poetry written in English. The opening and closing lines in each stanza, the refrain, begin with an iamb: I know (de-dum). The central lines start with two unstressed beats (de-de-dum), called an anapaest.

When the **sun** is **bright** on the **up**land **slopes**
De-de-dum de-dum de-de-dum de-dum

Leah says …

This is not just a dry exercise in scanning rhythm to trot out in an examination. Noticing changes in rhythm is of no use if it is not linked to reader response. What Dunbar does here so skilfully is to contrast an image of nature moving freely with the caged bird. The contrast is echoed in the change of rhythm and the change to a three-beat line to end each stanza.

Taster draft

Explain that the next stanzas will describe the caged bird juxtaposed with the landscape and the freedom it is denied. But before reading on, the children will write their own stanza in a **taster draft**!

The table on page 75 may help to scaffold their thinking. Display the techniques that Dunbar has employed in the first stanza as inspiration.

Your young writers may wish to include:

❦ Sight, sound, touch and smell.

❦ Repeated sounds (will they be soft or harsh?).

❦ A simile that speaks of entrapment.

❦ Carefully chosen verbs of movement (free or restricted?).

❦ Nouns that contrast with the rich perfume, glass and chalice of the first stanza.

They might need a launching point, so provide the opening line to the second stanza:

I know why the caged bird beats his wing …

Encourage the children to add as many ideas to the middle column as possible and then swap with a partner. Which ideas do they think are the most powerful? Ask the readers to help the writers by adding to the third column – what does the description imply about the bird?

Aspects of the bird	Description	Implying or symbolising ...
Perch		
Bars/cage		
Wings		
Feet		
Song		

You can then ask reader–writer pairs to share what they feel is their most powerful idea with the whole group, making evaluation a regular habit.

The rhythm and rhyme scheme are vital to Dunbar's dignified protest. Can your pupils replicate this? You might not insist on it, but why put a cap on possibility? Make sure to have rhyming dictionaries out on all desks and provide a version of the first stanza on which the lines have been scanned – the heavy stresses are marked in the example that follows on page 76. This will speak volumes to those who feel they want to meet the challenge of exploring poetry's prosody (its musical dimensions) in their own writing.

I know what the caged bird feels, alas!

When the sun is bright on the upland slopes;

When the wind stirs soft through the springing grass,

And the river flows like a stream of glass;

When the first bird sings and the first bud opes,

And the faint perfume from its chalice steals –

I know what the caged bird feels!

Reading journeys

Your pupils will now have understood, through interweaving reading and writing, the central, poignant symbol of the poem and how it expresses pain through contrast. This should create confidence and focus for how Dunbar takes his poem forward.

You can now reveal the full text:

Sympathy

I know what the caged bird feels, alas!

When the sun is bright on the upland slopes;

When the wind stirs soft through the springing grass,

And the river flows like a stream of glass;

    When the first bird sings and the first bud opes,

And the faint perfume from its chalice steals –

I know what the caged bird feels!

I know why the caged bird beats his wing

    Till its blood is red on the cruel bars;

For he must fly back to his perch and cling

When he fain would be on the bough a-swing;

    And a pain still throbs in the old, old scars

And they pulse again with a keener sting –

I know why he beats his wing!

I know why the caged bird sings, ah me,

    When his wing is bruised and his bosom sore, –

When he beats his bars and he would be free;

It is not a carol of joy or glee,

    But a prayer that he sends from his heart's deep core,

But a plea, that upward to Heaven he flings –

I know why the caged bird sings!

Having written their own version of the poem, invite the children to talk about what surprises them and what moves them. Readers of all ages need space for authentic, personal responses.

Leah says ...

I find it energising and refreshing to read Barbara Bleiman's (2018) comments on the links between word knowledge and reading. A teacher keen to support their pupils to understand the power of poetic techniques and contextual history can be in danger of supplanting authentic responses with mere information. What Bleiman advises are journeys in which all pupils are encouraged to make connections and develop responses, so that an exploration of writerly techniques can deepen rather than replace critical understanding. Engage with the whole, and how the parts relate to the whole.

Your readers deserve now to know something of Dunbar, theoretically a free black American citizen but who felt and saw around him the ghosts of slavery in the treatment of people of colour. We will call this **cueing in context**. You may wish to display or hand out some key biographical details. There are excellent biographies at https://www. poetryfoundation.org/poets/paul-laurence-dunbar/ and https:// www.poets.org/poetsorg/poet/paul-laurence-dunbar.

A well-focused, research-based homework would work well at this point: Paul Laurence Dunbar was born in 1872 in the northern state of Ohio, after the American Civil War. He was the son of Joshua and Mathilda Dunbar, freed slaves from the southern state of Kentucky.

❦ Why would a free man write this poem?

❦ What other kinds of 'cage' might he have suffered?

The group should now be ready for a deep, personal, critical and contextualised second read of the poem. As ever, let the pupils discuss their responses to the big question first. They will gain confidence from the shared dialogic struggle. **Radial questions** can be used as contingent scaffolds for small group focused responses or as open access. See figure on page 80.

Leah says ...

Albert Bandura is an influential social cognitive psychologist who pioneered research into self-efficacy (how we build confidence in a particular subject domain). His central finding is that purposeful struggle which leads to new insights anchors a learning experience in the memory. It is the memory of having done well that builds true efficacy: 'That was a struggle, but I worked through it, and I can remember what helped.'

Excellent responses will include:

Key concept: symbolic meaning through contrast

❦ How difficult it is to read and comment on the continued beating of the bird's wings when they are bruised and red with blood and its bosom sore. Dunbar makes us confront this with no comment. Your young readers may well be horrified, but are they also impressed by the bird's refusal to be still?

❦ The control and dignity maintained in this lyrical voice in the face of indignity.

79

Support:
Why does Dunbar begin with the gentle, sensory description of the landscape, before describing the caged bird?

Support:
How many beats per line are there?
Look carefully at the final line of each stanza: why are they shorter even though they repeat the first line?

Support:
Why might Dunbar finish the poem with a reference to the caged bird's song? How would you feel now listening to the song of a caged bird?

How does Paul Laurence Dunbar convey the suffering and determination of the caged bird?

Support:
Compare the verbs and the noun phrases used in the first stanza with those in the second.

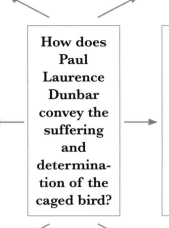

Support:
Why does the caged bird keep beating its wings when its old scars throb and it is bruised and sore?

Greater depth:
Who are the 'caged birds' in our own society?
Does this poem suggest that there is hope for those who cannot sing of 'joy or glee'?

❦ The movement verbs in the second and third stanzas ('beats', 'throbs', 'pulse') contrast with the free and gentle verbs in the first stanza ('stirs', 'flows', 'opes', 'steals'). Is there a ray of hope in the final prayer that the bird 'sends' and 'flings'?

❦ The powerful metaphor of the caged bird's song.

Key concept: structure supports meaning

❦ The stanza sequence being crucial to the shocking contrast at the core of the poem.

❦ The shortened final lines – three beats compared to four – bring the reader to an abrupt, poignant pause at the end of each stanza and the end of the poem.

Beyond the limit – link reading

Maya Angelou – poet, writer, editor, actor, dancer and civil rights activist – took Dunbar's final line as the title for her first autobiography: *I Know Why the Caged Bird Sings*. Having suffered abuse as a child, she was an elective mute for five years of her life. She lived through her reading and was only persuaded to speak by a teacher and mentor who convinced her that you don't really love poetry until you speak it. What do your pupils think about this claim? Angelou's poem 'Caged Bird' (published in 1983) provides a fascinating modern contrast to 'Sympathy'. Is the song of the caged bird different in the later poem?

Leah says ...

How about offering a range of link reading as an anthology and asking pairs or groups to prepare an oral reading of the poem that means most to them? Can they bring out the power of contrast in their reading?

Civil rights poetry continuing the theme of birds and song:

- ❧ 'Caged Bird' by Maya Angelou
- ❧ 'When I Rise Up' by Georgia Douglas Johnson
- ❧ 'The Gift to Sing' by James Weldon Johnson

Animals and freedom:

- ❧ 'Alys at the Zoo' by Raymond Garlick
- ❧ 'The Jaguar' by Ted Hughes
- ❧ 'How to Paint the Portrait of a Bird' by Jacques Prévert

Poetry from the American civil rights movement:

- ❧ 'Still I Rise' by Maya Angelou
- ❧ 'I, Too' by Langston Hughes
- ❧ 'To America' by James Weldon Johnson

If you would like to build contemporary knowledge of the context in which Dunbar was writing, Sojourner Truth's speeches offer an insight into the United States that Dunbar's parents would have been born into. As a freed woman she became an activist for racial and gender equality through public speaking, song and legal action. There is an excellent website that archives authentic versions of her speeches: https://sojournertruthmemorial.org/sojourner-truth/her-words/.

Within Shaun Usher's powerful collection *Speeches of Note* sit many lesser known speeches by African-Americans from the time of slavery, through the civil rights movement and beyond to our own times when freedom should be a universal right and yet is still something too many are fighting for. 'What to the Slave is the Fourth of July?' by Frederick Douglass and 'We Are All Bound Up Together' by Frances Harper are just two of many examples.

Wings to fly

Ask the children to write their own poem which uses contrast to highlight injustice.

- Having read 'Sympathy' and Angelou's 'Caged Bird', you might take up the image of the caged bird to speak of the inequality and injustice you see in your own life or culture. Will you borrow their powerful structure, introducing your poem with the symbols of freedom that others are denied? Why does your caged bird sing? What does it sing of? Will it be heard?

- Write about someone you know who is 'caged'. We can be caged by our own fears, by opportunity, by poverty or by prejudice. Maurice Williamson's 'Be Ye Not Afraid' speech to the New Zealand Parliament in 2013 would open doors to writing about LGBT (lesbian, gay, bisexual and transgender) rights.

- Depict two strong images of people or places which, simply by being placed together, speak of inequality or injustice.

Unit 6

Over It Dashes a Waterfall

'A Coloured Print by Shokei'
by Amy Lowell

Opening Doors key strategy: facts and feelings

Can you understand how a picture can be described with emotion?

Show how well you can write when stimulated by visual inspiration.

Have you ever stared at a painting, a print or a picture in a book and let your imagination fly? Has the picture begun to mean something to you as you've gazed at it? Has it raised questions or made you think of stories linked with the image?

Amy Lowell's poem 'A Coloured Print by Shokei' provides a top-class vehicle for exploring how poets fuse fact and emotion, as a description of an ancient Japanese print brings a personal interpretation alive in words. Can your pupils explore a painting and do the same?

Born in Boston, Massachusetts in 1874, Amy Lowell went on to become a poet and was posthumously awarded the Pulitzer Prize for

Poetry in 1926. She is associated with the imagist movement which valued visual clarity and the precise use of language. Imagists often wrote in **free verse** – an open form of poetry which relaxes the need for specific metrical patterns. Lowell wrote 'A Coloured Print by Shokei' in 1912.

How can the theme of this poem be accessed? In the 'Opening Doors' series, we often advocate that pupils learn in stages about the themes, challenges and big questions in a text. This work may be complemented by images, drama or slivers of text which explore the wonder of the writing that is slowly being revealed and understood. However, this time we're going to suggest something different.

Lowell's poem hinges on the revelation in the final stanza that the stunning view is actually a print, so we think a more formal reading of the whole poem is needed. You could perhaps withhold the title at first – in this way, your pupils will enjoy the reading without knowing that it is about a print until you reach the final stanza.

There are two other strategies that might help with the reception of the poem:

1. Specifically ask the children to think about the importance of the ending.

2. Instead of asking questions or exploring themes immediately after the reading, get your pupils to draw the waterfall scene. This activity will encourage them to engross themselves in the poem and to keep referring back to the vocabulary and context.

You have the illustration to show to any pupils who are stuck, plus this web page shows the likely print by Yamada Shokei of Nikko Waterfall from his 'Album of the True Views of Japan' (*c*.1892): https://www.ohmigallery.com/DB/ItemDetail.asp?item=8715.

Reading journeys

Resource 22

A Coloured Print by Shokei

It winds along the face of a cliff
    This path which I long to explore,
And over it dashes a waterfall,
    And the air is full of the roar
And the thunderous voice of waters which sweep
In a silver torrent over some steep.

It clears the path with a mighty bound
    And tumbles below and away,
And the trees and the bushes which grow in the rocks
    Are wet with its jewelled spray;
The air is misty and heavy with sound,
And small, wet wildflowers star the ground.

Oh! The dampness is very good to smell.
    And the path is soft to tread,
And beyond the fall it winds up and on,
    While little streamlets thread

Support:
Which words or phrases imply emotions and responses rather than factual descriptions?

Support:
Link any two of the emotive phrases together and discuss their meaning (e.g. 'mighty bound' and 'thunderous voice').

What does Amy Lowell feel as well as see as she looks at the print? Explore the ways in which she writes her own 'painting' in words.

Support:
Collect and discuss any images which appeal to the senses (e.g. 'heavy with sound').

Greater depth:
Compare the way any other two poems both describe a scene and introduce feelings and responses. Which is your favourite and why?

Their own meandering way down the hill

Each singing its own little song, until

I forget that 't is only a pictured path,

    And I hear the water and wind,

And look through the mist, and strain my eyes

    To see what there is behind;

For it must lead to a happy land,

This little path by a waterfall spanned.

Use the 'Opening Doors' challenge question (on page 88) to encourage your pupils to go deeper with their thinking. There are support questions, too, for those who need them.

Another useful method is to set up an **inform and infer** group talk session. Give each group a different image to explore: what associations do they have with each image and what is being inferred? The following table provides some examples – the left-hand column should be a fact and the right-hand column should be a cue to search for meaning between the lines.

Inform	Infer – explore further
A path winds around a cliff face	'happy land'

Inform	Infer – explore further
A powerful waterfall plunges over the path	'silver torrent'

Ask each group to come up with synonyms for the words in the 'infer' column and take feedback on their suggestions. Ask questions about spelling patterns and word **morphology** – for example, encourage the children to write down anything connected with 'torrent' and 'silver' – it will be a trail of discovery! This can include teaching them about spelling patterns and structures.

There are many more images in the poem to talk about in depth. All the texts in the 'Opening Doors' series give opportunities to teach spelling, punctuation and grammar in context as issues arise within a healthy questioning classroom environment.

Bob says ...

The key is the text itself! Use Amy Lowell's image-making to maximum learning effect. Only a demanding text can produce the deepest learning, but the content needs to open doors in the mind first.

Use the following success criteria to inform your expectations about pupil progress.

Excellent responses will:

Key concept: narrator's 'voice'

❦ Provide detailed explanations of figures of speech, like the metaphor 'jewelled spray'.

❦ Show how the figures of speech reflect emotions and personal responses, not just identify them.

❦ Link images together to show coherence and explain the exact meaning of each one. They might be linked around senses, emotions or the 'happy land' theme.

The poem makes me (Bob) reflect on personal experiences: the view of a mountain, an empty beach, the sound of a river or stream. How does what I see immediately link with what I feel? There are some famous Wordsworth quotes about poetry, in particular this one from the preface to *Lyrical Ballads* (2013: 111): 'Poetry is the spontaneous overflow of powerful feelings: it takes its origin from emotion recollected in tranquillity.'

Amy Lowell's poem also reminds me of these famous lines from Wordsworth's 'I Wandered Lonely as a Cloud' – they may be the lines of poetry that people are most familiar with!

For oft, when on my couch I lie
In vacant or in pensive mood,
They flash upon that inward eye
Which is the bliss of solitude;

And then my heart with pleasure fills,
And dances with the daffodils.

We can think about any moment when a sight and an emotion have worked concurrently in the brain. You could compare the children's responses here with those to 'Cold Mountain' (Unit 4) when the poet is actually on the mountain range.

Some of your pupils may not have experienced the countryside, so this could be an opportunity to take them there. Alternatively, apply the same principle to the sights and sounds of local life. How can an apparently factual description be crafted into something imaginative by poetry?

Since 1976, the children's author Michael Morpurgo has run a scheme called Farms for City Children with his wife, Clare: https://farmsforcitychildren.org. The charity offers urban children the opportunity to live and work on a real farm in the heart of the countryside.

Beyond the limit – link reading

These poems can be part of the richer curriculum provision for this unit's **deep objective**. Try to find curriculum time for the children to choose, browse and make links with other texts, as well as some explicit teaching about ways in which the 'voice' in Amy Lowell's poem takes the view of the artwork way beyond an emotionally detached description. Remember though that the voice of the narrator in a poem is not necessarily that of the poet themselves.

- ❦ 'The Pleiades' and 'A Japanese Wood Carving' by Amy Lowell
- ❦ 'Brueghel's Winter' by Walter de la Mare
- ❦ 'The Path' by Edward Thomas (Unit 5 in *Opening Doors to Famous Poetry and Prose*)
- ❦ 'The Lake Isle of Innisfree' by W. B. Yeats
- ❦ 'The Pied Piper of Hamelin' by Robert Browning (Unit 18 in *Opening Doors to Famous Poetry and Prose*)
- ❦ 'How to Paint the Portrait of a Bird' by Jacques Prévert
- ❦ *Lost Horizon* by James Hilton

Wings to fly

When I (Bob) first found this poem, quite recently, I was struck by the last two lines:

For it must lead to a happy land,
This little path by a waterfall spanned.

There are many metaphorical associations with paths (as explored in Unit 5 of *Opening Doors to Famous Poetry and Prose*). I love the idea of a 'little path' leading to something momentous, something figurative or maybe something real. In the **link reading**, which will deepen your pupils' reading experiences, I have included a famous prose work, James Hilton's *Lost Horizon*, because the travellers' journey to Shangri-La after a plane crash captures the idea of a spiritual place in the mountains where, perhaps, mankind can prosper and live to an incredible old age.

Your pupils should enjoy writing about that supposed 'happy land' or any other kind of variation they create from looking at any painting. Writing advice could include learning from Lowell's techniques and crafting **taster drafts** of a poem which describe the emotional feelings brought on by seeing a work of art. Let the pen flow quickly, though, or the writing could become too self-conscious.

The children should imitate Lowell's appeal to the senses to come up with some original metaphors and use their link reading experiences to deepen the creative possibilities. For example, what kind of land did the piper take the children to in 'The Pied Piper of Hamelin'? Can they find the Brueghel painting referred to by Walter de la Mare?

Which of these titles appeal to your class?

- The Small Path to the Happy Land
- The Small Path to a Dangerous Land
- The Waterfall of Jewels
- Search for the following paintings and write a poem which both describes what you see and also expresses your emotions:
  - *The Hunters in the Snow* by Pieter Brueghel the Elder
  - *Water Lilies* by Claude Monet
  - *The Scream* by Edvard Munch
  - *A Wheatfield with Cypresses* by Vincent Van Gogh

  Or for a city scene:
  - *VE Day – 1945* by L. S. Lowry

❦ The Path Which I Long to Explore ... Here is your chance – it could be any type of path, literal or figurative!

Creative thinking on any of these titles will go further if supported by searching online for landscape paintings by Piet Mondrian, Wassily Kandinsky or Charles Rennie Mackintosh.

There is a quote attributed to Leonardo da Vinci which provides a useful way to reflect further on this unit: 'Painting is poetry that is seen rather than felt. Poetry is painting that is felt rather than seen.' Perhaps your pupils may have merged the two with a little inspiration from Amy Lowell!

Unit 7

Old King Time!

'Song of Old Time' by Eliza Cook

Opening Doors key strategy: major motifs

How well can you make links on a key idea through a poem and across poems?

How successful can your key idea be in an anthology of poems?

Access strategies

What puzzles you about the illustration? Can you think of a theme suggested by it?

Eliza Cook is a Victorian poet who has written a haunting poem about the power of time which would make any reader reflect on their own day-to-day concerns. We love the ending best:

But the marble shall crumble, the pillar shall fall,
And Time, Old Time, will be king after all.

This could be a good starting point for the children to access the text:

❦ What do you associate with 'king'?

❦ Why is 'Old Time' capitalised?

❦ What might the crumbling marble represent?

Time, as a proper noun, is often perceived to be overlooking, or even controlling, the affairs of mankind. One such example is the weather vane at Lord's Cricket Ground in London (a quick internet search will turn up lots of images). Of course, Father Time often carries an hour-glass and a scythe. Time can only move one way – forward! The scythe is a symbol linked with death – the Grim Reaper who comes to reap the dead, just like a crop. These are motifs with powerful associations. The children can learn how writers manipulate these motifs for creativity and meaning-making.

Explore with your pupils how personification and the **extended metaphor** of Time's power seeps through the imagery. Offer them a sliver of text:

I eat through treasures with moth and rust;

I lay the gorgeous palace in dust;

I make the shell-proof tower my own,

And break the battlement, stone from stone.

Resource 24

This is King Time indeed!

Get the children to work on a **mark and note** exercise. Stick a print-out of the four lines to the centre of a sheet of flipchart paper and prompt the pupils to note down questions, themes, inspirations or enquiries; without this guidance, there is a risk that it will simply become a 'naming of parts' exercise.

Alternatively, set some specific tasks for exploration:

- ❦ Debate the importance of the verbs linked with the first-person voice, like 'lay' or 'break'. Can you offer any alternatives?

- ❦ Why is it important that material things seem attractive? Think about 'treasure' or 'gorgeous' as an adjective.

A **taster draft** should produce some original images and deepen your pupils' understanding of extending a metaphor and creating momentum in a poem. Ask them to write four lines on the themes they have identified in Eliza Cook's poem. Which verbs will they use? Which material, buildings or possessions will be seen decaying?

You could introduce some of the **link reading** at this point, especially Charlotte Brontë's 'Mementos' (Unit 9 in *Opening Doors to Quality Writing for Ages 10 to 13*). She uses some striking images of decay which will help to feed their ideas. Shelley's 'Ozymandias' is world famous and makes a striking impression on the vanity of human power and self-worship.

As with all taster drafts, there are huge opportunities in the assessment for learning session (which can take the form of a **mini-plenary**) for evaluation, comparison and advice. We find that pupils listen with more focus than when summative assessments are simply marked and discussed. They really appreciate that this is an opportunity to improve their writing and develop their spelling skills, because errors are collated and corrected. The classroom can have a vibrant workshop atmosphere! The draft writing will improve the children's comprehension when Eliza Cook's poem is revealed in full.

Reading journeys

Song of Old Time

I wear not the purple of earth-born kings,
Nor the stately ermine of lordly things;
But monarch and courtier, though great they be,
Must fall from their glory and bend to me.
My sceptre is gemless; yet who can say
They will not come under its mighty sway?
Ye may learn who I am,– there's the passing chime,
And the dial to herald me, Old King Time!

Softly I creep, like a thief in the night,
After cheeks all blooming and eyes all light;
My steps are seen on the patriarch's brow,
In the deep-worn furrows and locks of snow.
Who laughs at my power? The young and gay;
But they dream not how closely I track their way.

Wait till their first bright sands have run,
And they will not smile at what Time hath done.

I eat through treasures with moth and rust;
I lay the gorgeous palace in dust;
I make the shell-proof tower my own,
And break the battlement, stone from stone.
Work on at your cities and temples, proud man,
Build high as ye may, and strong as ye can;
But the marble shall crumble, the pillar shall fall,
And Time, Old Time, will be king after all.

The challenging 'Opening Doors' question that follows on page 102 can be set quite quickly because the pupils will have already learnt so much from their taster drafts and explorations. However, the support questions can prompt further **direct transmission** if there are any gaps in their knowledge that need to be filled (e.g. vocabulary like 'sceptre' or 'courtier'). **Dialogic talk** may be more effective for other questions – for example, why is a 'patriarch' chosen to illustrate a 'deep-worn furrow'?

You may want to teach more about tone by comparing 'Song of Old Time' with Units 1 or 3. Any stylistic matters are best taught via examples and link reading because it makes them easier to discuss – for example, the tone of authority in stanza one and increasing arrogance or boastfulness in stanza two.

Support:

Which examples show Time relishing his power? Choose two favourite sections and say why you like them.

Support:

Write about the tone of the poem. How does it develop stanza by stanza? Create a table with the content listed on the left and tone on the right.

How has Eliza Cook imaginatively expressed the power of Old King Time?

Support:

Why is the poem called a 'song'? How does the rhyming contribute to the universal theme? Recite the poem and practise how to express the theme dramatically.

Greater depth:

Compare the way Time claims to be king in 'Song of Old Time' with Shelley's famous poem 'Ozymandias'. A table of similarities and differences will support your thinking. You could consider content, tone and images separately to make a start.

Your key strategy for 'Opening Doors' is to unpack all the ways that poets like Eliza Cook select a combination of words to express universal truths.

Bob says ...

In all our ' Opening Doors' work, we recommend finding the best methodology to suit the objective. This may involve an element of trial and error - which is why having so many tools in the toolkit is critical. However, it is the richness of the text that will give you the space and opportunities you need to teach more and to teach deeply.

Excellent responses will:

Key concept: personification

- ❦ Explore and explain how the personification of Time builds through the poem, particularly as the tone becomes more savage.

- ❦ Show how the images combine to reveal the ravages that Time inflicts.

- ❦ Include examples of how the 'Song of Old Time' looks on mankind's 'rule' with disdain.

The high-pitched success criteria is primarily designed to stimulate teachers' thinking about the knowledge to be acquired for reading and understanding the poem. The statements have no life as a discrete list. They are for you to utilise in your lessons, and perhaps to consider with your teaching team about what you might expect pupils to write when going deeper towards mastery.

Bob says ...

If accessed well, literary texts have deep learning potential. Your pupils can acquire more vocabulary, more knowledge and more experience of stylistic ranges than in less demanding texts. The excellent success criteria can be a way of jump-starting your own reflections about the kinds of learning and knowledge you need to prioritise in your own teaching.

One of the major messages in John Hattie's influential *Visible Learning for Teachers* (2012: 39) is the power to be gained by teachers 'critiquing each other, planning together, evaluating together, and finding many other ways to work together'. We suggest that teaching teams should, as a habit, discuss potential first-class excellence criteria as a way of learning more about texts. This is ongoing curriculum design work – and is the opposite of passively accepting someone else's package.

By putting quality texts at the centre of the curriculum, teachers are giving themselves daily continuing professional development in a self-reflective and ad hoc way. So much more happens in a classroom with quirky, challenging reading! We learn less from standard 'safe' resources than we do from the deep enquiry that comes from using texts like 'Song of Old Time', 'A Coloured Print by Shokei' or *David Copperfield*.

In her book *The Curriculum: Gallimaufry to Coherence*, Mary Myatt (2018: 26) states: 'We need to stop being squeamish about talking about scholarship, deep learning and our pupils having access to and mastering robust knowledge.' 'Opening Doors' schools are telling us that in a sense knowledge is power – and teachers are accumulating more of it too. However, a whole toolkit of learning skills is needed to unpack the ways in which that knowledge can be acquired and applied.

Beyond the limit – link reading

The theme of Time has preoccupied poets for centuries. These poems are classics by anyone's definition:

- ❦ 'Mementos' by Charlotte Brontë (Unit 9 in *Opening Doors to Quality Writing for Ages 10 to 13*)
- ❦ 'Time, You Old Gipsy Man' by Ralph Hodgson (available at https://www.bartleby.com/103/109.html)
- ❦ 'Cities and Thrones and Powers' by Rudyard Kipling
- ❦ 'To His Coy Mistress' by Andrew Marvell
- ❦ 'Ozymandias' by Percy Bysshe Shelley
- ❦ 'The Both of Us' by Joshua Seigel
- ❦ 'Tomorrow, and Tomorrow, and Tomorrow' speech from *Macbeth* by William Shakespeare
- ❦ 'Fern Hill' by Dylan Thomas

'Ozymandias' is a good poem to include in the greater depth work. The children could compare the 'vast and trunkless legs of stone' seen by the traveller, with the cry of, 'Look on my Works, ye Mighty, and despair!' Can your pupils track a similar theme about the transience of power in 'Song of Old Time'? It seems that the Egyptian pharaoh Ramesses II was the inspiration for Shelley's poem: he had a statue of himself made bearing the inscription, 'King of Kings am I, Ozymandias'. Is it humbling or scary to know how harshly Time may judge us?

Wings to fly

Time is a great subject to write about. Encourage your pupils to apply what the works of Eliza Cook, Percy Bysshe Shelley, Rudyard Kipling and Dylan Thomas have taught them to devise their own poem on one of these themes:

- Song of Old Mother Time
- My Encounter with Father Time on the River of Life
- Write about any of these topics to show Time bringing destruction and change:
  - A cliff
  - The bottom of the sea
  - A single road or house
- Invent a new figure for Time which is different from Father Time. Can you think of something other than an hourglass for the figure to carry? Give the character a personality.
- Continue a poem using these starters from your reading:
  - I met a traveller from an antique land who said …
  - I eat through treasures with moth and rust ….
  - Time let me play and be …
  - Golden in the mercy of his means …
  - I used to be an estuary but now I'm just a brook …

❦ All things I'll give you ...

❦ Will you be my guest ...

If any of your pupils are stuck, some potential structures might be:

✓ A new tone for each stanza.

✓ A new stage of Time's power for each stanza.

✓ A draft personality profile for Time.

An endnote for this unit can go to Rudyard Kipling. It may help your pupils to grasp a difficult concept for the young – that all ideas and civilisations will one day give way to others:

Cities and Thrones and Powers
   Stand in Time's eye,
Almost as long as flowers,
   Which daily die.

Unit 8

Zoom in

'The Dong with a Luminous Nose' by Edward Lear

Opening Doors key strategy: using camera angles to structure writing

What is the effect of using different perspectives of the same setting in writing?

Can you use shifts in perspective to build mood in your own writing?

Children are becoming increasingly familiar with narrative in films as the use of this medium becomes ever more accessible at home and in school. Whilst many adults may despair at the shift from the active to the on-screen in learning and leisure, we can, as teachers, use this to our advantage. After all, even our youngest pupils will be familiar, even if only at a subconscious level, with the way a storyline unfolds or how moods can be created through a series of camera angles.

Let's start with some well-known films – for example, the opening sequence of Disney's *The Lion King* (see https://www.youtube.com/watch?v=GibiNy4d4gc). The first, wide-angle shot of the blazing African planes immediately provides an overall understanding of the setting. What then follows is a sequence of medium- and wide-angle shots that develop a feeling for the vastness of the environment, until finally there is a close-up of the Lion King, Mufasa, which indicates to the audience that he is an important character. Over the sequence, the director invites the audience to shift from a wide to a narrow gaze.

The first thirty seconds of *Pirates of the Caribbean: The Curse of the Black Pearl* (see https://www.youtube.com/watch?v=dfPYuI1cBpc) uses the same technique to build a mood of mystery and suspense. The wide-angle view of a misty sea is followed by the progressively closer and closer shot of a ship, finally resting with a close-up of the face of a singing child on what seems to be a deserted deck. We know the setting, we know the character and we know that something is about to happen to this young girl!

Year 5 pupils at Westbury Park Primary School in Bristol spent three weeks of the autumn term exploring how these strategies could be used in suspense writing. Inspired by the opening sequence from *Pirates of the Caribbean,* Joe zooms in on a character on the lonely deck of the world's first great passenger ship, the *SS Great Britain,* during one of its Atlantic journeys in the early 1800s.

Black, just black, blacker than the blackest black; whilst darkness filtered the light the moon casted sinister shadows onto the vile twisted buildings of Bristol which seemed to cackle viciously in the wind as though enjoying this vast, cold, indefatigable silence.

And now, a boat majestic but spectral its bow slicing through the silent slumbering night. Flags rippled desperately on its corpse-like masts, hissing and groaning in the stinging air, which lashed and crashed against the cowering surface of the vast ship encased in its claw-like cage of effervescent glass.

We zoom in more to a window, and behind this window there seemed to be a shape …

Joe Stephenson

If you don't have access to these particular films, there are many others which work in the same way – starting with a wide-angle shot to set the scene, followed by closer shots as important details are introduced and the mood is set. Challenge pupils to look for this strategy in their own viewing and think about why the director might have used it. Be aware that it is not only used at the start of films but also if a new location is introduced. For example, in Danny DeVito's adaptation of *Matilda* (1996), the same shift between wide, medium and close-up angles is employed for over twenty seconds when Miss Trunchbowl's school is initially introduced.

Verity says …

Using the familiar medium of film is a great way into thinking about narrative structure. It allows pupils to experience quickly a sense of structure through both the visual and audio before tackling a written text.

You may want to use some of the linked reading ideas here: bringing in short examples of the zoom-in approach early will open the pupils' eyes to how film-makers use techniques from literature.

Reading journeys

Having done the preparatory work, let's start the **reading journey**. Give the class the first three stanzas of Edward Lear's 'The Dong with a Luminous Nose', but mix them up and omit the title. Can the pupils work out which order they go in and why? Ask them to consider how Lear has used the same strategies that film directors use to set the scene and mood in his poetry – starting with a wide angle and gradually zooming in to a particular character.

Resource 27

When awful darkness and silence reign
Over the great Gromboolian plain,
Through the long, long wintry nights; –
When the angry breakers roar
As they beat on the rocky shore; –
When Storm-clouds brood on the towering heights
Of the Hills of the Chankly Bore: –

Then, through the vast and gloomy dark,
There moves what seems a fiery spark,
A lonely spark with silvery rays
Piercing the coal-black night, –
A Meteor strange and bright: –
Hither and thither the vision strays,
A single lurid light.

Slowly it wanders, – pauses, – creeps, –

Anon it sparkles, – flashes and leaps;

And ever as onward it gleaming goes

A light on the Bong-tree stems it throws.

And those who watch at that midnight hour

From Hall or Terrace, or lofty Tower,

Cry, as the wild light passes along, –

'The Dong! – the Dong!

'The wandering Dong through the forest goes!

'The Dong! the Dong!

'The Dong with a luminous Nose!'

Using a blank storyboard of three squares, ask the pupils to draw the three images portrayed in each of the stanzas. This will enable them to really think about the language and what it means. Make sure there is plenty of time to talk about language choice and vocabulary. Compare the children's storyboards and consider what imagery has been included most frequently: what are the common themes?

As a group, consider what it is about the poem that makes it so memorable, mysterious or funny.

Excellent responses will include:

Key concept: building tension

❦ Starting from far away and zooming in to an amusing final line – who would have expected the creature to have a luminous nose!

❦ The contrast of dark and light in the second stanza which provides mystery and tension.

Key concept: creating mood

❦ The sense of foreboding which is created in the first stanza where the setting is introduced. This is developed through the choice of language which includes personification and repetition: 'awful darkness', 'long, long wintry nights', 'angry breakers roar', 'storm clouds brood'.

❦ The use of dashes which slows down the rhythm and creates a clear image of what the creature is doing.

Having zoomed in from a wide angle to a close-up of the Dong in the first three stanzas, challenge the pupils to create a **taster draft** of a further stanza (or some prose) which describes this character in even more detail – an extreme close-up. We know he has a luminous nose but little else. This quick writing will really spark their imagination.

Now compare the pupils' work with Lear's original description:

A Nose as strange as a Nose could be!
Of vast proportions and painted red,

And tied with cords to the back of his head.

– In a hollow rounded space it ended

With a luminous Lamp within suspended,

All fenced about

With a bandage stout

To prevent the wind from blowing it out; –

And with holes all round to send the light,

In gleaming rays on the dismal night.

Mark and note is used as a strategy in Unit 15 of *Opening Doors to a Richer English Curriculum for Ages 6 to 9* on Andri Snær Magnason's *The Story of the Blue Planet*. The same technique can be used here to collect evidence relating to camera angles. The children can highlight words or phrases that they may be unsure of, or want to celebrate, and then share questions such as:

❧ Why has the author used the nose as the focus for the character?

❧ Why has darkness been used as the setting?

❧ How difficult would it be to see the Dong?

The storyboards and texts used or created through this work could be developed further as a cross-curricular project using apps such as Movie Maker or I Can Animate. The artwork will come to life as pupils practise their oracy skills and recite the poem as a voiceover.

Beyond the limit – link reading

On the theme of unusual creatures, watching David Attenborough's *Blue Planet* never ceases to amaze. Your young readers could also draw on readings from picture books including:

- *The Land of Neverbelieve* by Norman Messenger
- *Fantastic Beasts and Where to Find Them* by J. K. Rowling (illustrated by Olivia Lomenech Gill)
- *Where the Wild Things Are* by Maurice Sendak
- *The Lost Thing* by Shaun Tan
- *The Mysteries of Harris Burdick* by Chris Van Allsburg
- *Flotsam* by David Wiesner

There are plenty of examples of both poetry and prose that you could introduce to your pupils to help them become more familiar with this technique of moving from a wider view to close-up:

- Compare the first six lines of Nicola Davies' poem *King of the Sky* with the accompanying four pages of illustrations by Laura Carlin. The same techniques have been employed: starting with a wide-angle view of rain on a hill, zooming into the picture line by line and finishing with a lonely figure.

- The first four lines of William Wordsworth's 'I Wandered Lonely As a Cloud'.

- The first three paragraphs of Richard Adams' *Watership Down* follows this same pattern but in prose. It starts with the wide-angle shot of the meadow before gradually zooming in to just two rabbits.

🐦 The first two paragraphs at the start of Part 4 of the prologue to Nahoko Uehashi's *The Beast Player*, which quickly moves from a starry night to a close-up of a woman with fireflies dancing over her head.

🐦 The first sighting of Moby Dick in Herman Melville's classic text draws the reader in from the open sea to a pointing motionless arm.

🐦 The opening of Morris Gleitzman's *Once* shifts from a mountainside, to an orphanage lunch table and to a whole carrot in some soup in just twenty-three lines!

Verity says ...

Short, well-chosen extracts are crucial to exploring literature. We don't always have a lot of time so it's essential that we use really rich examples. Quite often, I will use a short extract from a book that we don't have time to use as a class reader. However, this is often enough to whet the appetite of many young learners who then go on to read the complete text independently. This linked reading not only reinforces the strategies under scrutiny, but also offers pupils wider engagement with some great writers and opens the door to reading for pleasure just that little bit more.

If you want the children to think even more carefully about this technique, why not take a look at it being used in reverse and consider what the effect of such a strategy might be. Chapter 4 of John Boyne's *The Boy in the Striped Pyjamas* carefully describes what Bruno and his sister see outside their window, without realising that it is a concentration camp. Rather than beginning with a wide angle, Boyne starts describing what is close to Bruno's house, with each sentence panning out and taking the reader further and further away from the safe familiarity of the family home and into the unknown.

Using the same technique of zooming out, you could look at *Zoom* and the follow-up *Re-Zoom* by Istvan Banyai. These are incredibly clever picture books which take zooming out of a picture to a completely different level.

Wings to fly

Camera angles provide a simple and effective way of framing and structuring writing which is quickly grasped by young writers. It is also a good way of slowing down writing. Insisting that a wide angle is developed before zooming into the character and action ensures that detail is included.

There are many directions in which you could now take your pupils. You may want to give them different settings from which they can create an unusual creature who is moving through them. Refer back to the ways in which Lear's poem is successful. What choices will your writers make?

❦ Will it be a dark and scary setting that ends in amusement, or a welcoming setting that ends in something far darker?

❦ How will they create contrast?

- ❦ How will their creature move? What techniques can they use to convey this movement to the reader?
- ❦ Will there be a twist at the end?

Alternatively, the pupils could write from a different perspective and invert the poetry/prose they are using as inspiration: what would the Dong see from afar as he travels? What is in the distance and gets closer and closer?

Part 2

Opening Doors to Prose

Unit 9

Fifty Degrees Below Zero

'To Build a Fire' by Jack London

Opening Doors key strategy: a reader between the lines!

How does Jack London guide the reader's response to a dramatic narrative?

How well can you write a short story with the possibility of different versions and audiences?

Access strategies

Jack London is famous for his stories set in the frozen wastes of Alaska. By the end of the nineteenth century gold had been discovered, particularly in the area known as the Klondike. Jack London became a prospector and his stories introduced readers to a world of dog sleds, wolf packs, the wilderness, mining towns and, above all, the hazardous and freezing cold nature of the environment. They are classic adventure stories. Do take a look at Jack London's *That Spot* in *Opening Doors to Quality Writing for Ages 10 to 13* (Unit 3).

In fact, as we've mentioned in other units, you have the option of giving curriculum and home reading time to the **link reading** list at this stage. Even just browsing and beginning to read *White Fang* or *Call of the Wild* may be helpful before this in-depth study of 'To Build a Fire'. It also gives you a chance to say something about the Klondike Gold Rush. These links will help:

❦ https://jacklondonpark.com/jack-london-biography/

❦ https://www.literarytraveler.com/articles/jack_london_klondike/

William Grill's *Shackleton's Journey* may not be set in Alaska, but it's a superb non-fiction account and will give those who find the full London books hard a taste of how difficult travelling in any kind of frozen waste was in the past – and still is!

Read the opening paragraphs of the 1908 version of 'To Build a Fire' carefully for yourself to observe how the author has included clever clues and cues to the direction the story will take (there is a link on page 126). All of these cues help to open doors to questions and predictions in the mind: the narrative engages the reader with the growing feeling of danger.

Offer your pupils this sliver of text:

But all this – the mysterious, far-reaching hair-line trail, the absence of sun from the sky, the tremendous cold, and the strangeness and weirdness of it all – made no impression on the man.

Resource 30a

Tell your pupils nothing about Jack London's stories just yet; simply ask them to find and list the words that suggest the kind of environment where the story is set. More challenging is to ask each group to suggest why the phrase 'made no impression on the man' might be important to the coming narrative.

Now give your pupils the next sliver:

Resource 30b

> It was not because he was long used to it. He was a newcomer in the land, a *chechaquo*, and this was his first winter. The trouble with him was that he was without imagination. He was quick and alert in the things of life, but only in the things, and not in the significances.

Can your pupils predict the likely theme of the tale? Again, don't give them the title yet! The children's answers will be guesswork, but the best responses will be based on their comprehension of the small amount of information they have been given so far. It's the kind of practice that pupils need in order to become intrigued by the types of inferences to be found in stories. This will also give you the opportunity to explore with them what imagination means in the broadest sense. You could ask:

☙ How relevant will the 'newcomer' word be?

☙ What is someone like who is 'without imagination'? What does this imply?

☙ How does London make 'tremendous cold' stand out?

In this unit, you have the fascinating opportunity to compare the 1908 version of 'To Build a Fire' with the 1902 one, which was written for younger readers. Consider the much slimmer prose that London uses in the earlier version:

> The trail, which had seen little travel, followed the bed of the creek, and there was no possibility of his getting lost. He had gone to Dawson by way of Cherry Creek and Indian River, so Paul Creek was new and strange.

Both versions are available online: http://london.sonoma.edu/Writings/Uncollected/tobuildafire.html (1902) and https://americanenglish.state.gov/files/ae/resource_files/to-build-a-fire.pdf (1908).

Compare the same episode in both texts.

In the 1902 version, he stops to eat lunch:

> He had barely chewed the first mouthful when his numbing fingers warned him to put his mitten on again. This he did, not without surprise at the bitter swiftness with which the frost bit in. Undoubtedly it was the coldest snap he had ever experienced, he thought.

The 1908 version describes the same episode:

> He unbuttoned his jacket and drew forth his lunch. The action consumed no more than a quarter of a minute, yet in that brief moment the numbness laid hold of the exposed fingers. He did

not put the mitten on, but, instead, struck the fingers a dozen sharp smashes against his leg.

What do your pupils notice about the differences between the two versions? Get them to think about:

- ❦ Vocabulary
- ❦ Detail
- ❦ Key phrases
- ❦ Different audiences (the 1902 version was for an adventure magazine for boys)

Now that the children's understanding of the type of text they are engaging with is growing, insist on a **taster draft**. Some possible writing prompts could be to take key sentences from the more challenging (and more fascinating) 1908 version and ask for continuations. For example, expand this starter into a paragraph:

He should not have built the fire under the spruce tree. He should have built it in the open.

Discourage predictable narratives and encourage the building of tension – they are beginning to develop the big picture of the story.

Bob says ...

The best way to improve writing is to write, regularly! Get the children to write every day in short bursts on a range of quality texts. 'Opening Doors' schools are seeing some top-class examples which are often written in a short time and to a word limit.

Feedback can centre around any targeted aspect of spelling, punctuation or grammar in context. This is the great joy of taster drafts: your pupils will take advice from you, and from each other, on ways to create tension and infer meaning – and functional English contributes to that meaning too. The discussions you have on vocabulary will occur naturally and will be full of curiosity.

To go deeper, especially for peer review, you could use a **mark and note** strategy: ask the children to place questions or comments on sticky notes around passages from 'To Build a Fire' or the taster drafts. In 'Opening Doors' schools, we encourage teachers to get pupils to practise linking images and themes or find contrasts or **counterpoints**. This gives them more practice in understanding the overall meaning. Strategies could include marking the interesting contrasts or noting the warnings of potential danger. Follow this up with feedback on what has been noted and what kinds of evidence has been found.

Metacognitive strategies like this one provide the children with transferable skills and techniques. There is a key strategy for each unit. The Education Endowment Foundation has published an influential guidance report on *Metacognition and Self-Regulated Learning* which contains seven research-based recommendations (Quigley et al., 2019). The effectiveness of any strategy will be partly down to the teacher's feedback and advice, of course, so the pupils will internalise the need to develop such approaches, thereby making the learning intrinsic.

Reading journeys

You may now wish to give curriculum time to reading the whole short story. We would suggest the 1908 version, which will enable you to point out:

❦ The continued inference of catastrophe.

❦ The use of short topic sentences to signal anxiety.

❦ The comparison between the man and the dog.

❦ The descriptions of physical deterioration and increased desperation.

This is a story which provokes the reader's response paragraph by paragraph, line by line, word by word. We become completely involved with every action and every dramatic moment. If you read the text in an engaging way, you should see the pupils' emotions hit the surface.

Bob says ...

Your dramatic reading will be vital! How many memories do you have of your own teacher captivating your attention? It's magical.

Your thought-provoking questioning can then take their engagement deeper into the many ways in which London crafts his famous story. The 1902 version can certainly be explored as well – there is a much kinder ending! To delve into the differences between the two texts, which are aimed at different audiences, you could use the following passages and set a challenging question to open the doors to comprehension. As always, utilise the support and greater depth questions as appropriate.

1902:

By half past eleven he was at the forks, which had been described to him, and he knew he had covered fifteen miles, half the distance. He knew that in the nature of things the trail was bound to grow worse from there on, and thought that, considering the good time he had made, he merited lunch. Casting off his pack and taking a seat on a fallen tree, he unmittened his right hand, reached inside his shirt next to the skin, and fished out a couple of biscuits sandwiched with sliced bacon and wrapped in a handkerchief – the only way they could be carried without freezing solid.

He had barely chewed the first mouthful when his numbing fingers warned him to put his mitten on again. This he did, not without surprise at the bitter swiftness with which the frost bit in. Undoubtedly it was the coldest snap he had ever experienced, he thought.

1908:

He unbuttoned his jacket and shirt and drew forth his lunch. The action consumed no more than a quarter of a minute, yet in that brief moment the numbness laid hold of the exposed fingers. He did not put the mitten on, but, instead, struck the fingers a dozen sharp smashes against his leg. Then he sat down on a snow-covered log to eat. The sting that followed upon the striking of his fingers against his leg ceased so quickly that he was startled. He had had no chance to take a bite of biscuit. He struck the fingers repeatedly and returned them to the mitten, baring the other hand for the purpose of eating. He tried to take a mouthful, but the ice-muzzle prevented. He had forgotten to build a fire and thaw out.

1902:

After the first quick, biting sensation of cold, his feet had ached with a heavy, dull ache and were rapidly growing numb. But the fire, although a very young one, was now a success; he knew that a little snow, briskly rubbed, would speedily cure his feet.

But at the moment he was adding the first thick twigs to the fire a grievous thing happened. The pine boughs above his head were burdened with a four months snowfall, and so finely adjusted were the burdens that his slight movement in collecting the twigs had been sufficient to disturb the balance.

The snow from the topmost bough was the first to fall, striking and dislodging the snow on the boughs beneath. And all this snow, accumulating as it fell, smote Tom Vincent's head and shoulders and blotted out his fire.

1908:

But before he could cut the strings, it happened. It was his own fault or, rather, his mistake. He should not have built the fire under the spruce tree. He should have built it in the open. But it had been easier to pull the twigs from the brush and drop them directly on the fire. Now the tree under which he had done this carried a weight of snow on its boughs. No wind had blown for weeks, and each bough was fully freighted. Each time he had pulled a twig he had communicated a slight agitation to the tree – an imperceptible agitation, so far as he was concerned, but an agitation sufficient to bring about the disaster. High up in the tree one bough capsized its load of snow. This fell on the boughs beneath, capsizing them. This process continued, spreading out and involving the whole tree. It grew like an avalanche, and it descended without warning upon the man and the fire, and the fire was blotted out! Where it had burned was a mantle of fresh and disordered snow.

The man was shocked. It was as though he had just heard his own sentence of death.

Support:

Track the stages of anxiety as the man tries to eat his lunch. How are the sentences connected? Explore the feeling we get of the man's movements and frustration. How do you respond personally?

Support:

How does Jack London help the reader to visualise the two scenes?

What mistakes does the man make? How does this affect the way we respond to him?

How does Jack London use detail and drama in his 1908 narrative?

Support:

How does Jack London's knowledge of Alaska intensify the description of the fire going out? Consider:

• Noun phrases.

• The contrast between the factual account and the way the simile of the avalanche engages the reader.

Greater depth:

Compare extracts from the 1902 version and the 1908 version which describe the same moments. How has the different audience led to choices about style and vocabulary? Is Jack London a better writer in 1908?

An alternative route to understanding for those ready to study the whole story is to ask pupils to highlight in different colours the contrasting attitudes to the wilderness shown by the dog and the man. You can take this further by exploring how Jack London develops this ongoing tension.

Excellent responses will:

Key concept: guiding the reader's response

- Explain how step-by-step developments, often via the man's perspective, influence the reader's responses.
- Explore how the detail contributes to our responses: specific vocabulary, parts of speech, sentence length and the authenticity of the setting.
- Describe how key sentences or phrases turn the mounting atmosphere into the threat of danger.

Throughout the 'Opening Doors' series, we have emphasised how excellence criteria should be used by teachers in **dialogic talk** sessions, not as a to-do list for your pupils.

Bob says ...

Excellent responses guidelines are a key way in which assessment inspires a deeper curriculum and enables the next steps of learning to surface. Plan to use key concepts across the key stages to ensure there are multilayered possibilities and the potential for rich discussions for pupils of all abilities.

You could devise exercises to illustrate the step-by-step descriptions in this story. For example, a **mind link strategy** could support access by showing how sentences build towards a key moment or demonstrating how the man's false sense of confidence contrasts with the bitterly cold environment around him. The latter would be appropriate for large sections of the first part of 'To Build a Fire'.

Of course, you have free rein to use any parts of the story, not just the selected extracts. Older pupils may be more equipped to sift and sort across the story and make links in their minds. When you first read the whole story to the class you could stop at critical stages and ask them their views on the likelihood of the man's survival.

Beyond the limit – link reading

Choose the most appropriate time for linking in other whole texts to deepen pupils' responses. The following titles are all on the theme of frozen wastes:

- *The Snow Queen* by Hans Christian Andersen
- *Shackleton's Journey* by William Grill
- 'Cold Mountain' by Han-Shan (Unit 4)
- *The Lion, the Witch and the Wardrobe* by C. S. Lewis (winter scenes)
- *Northern Lights* by Philip Pullman
- 'Frost' and 'Daughter of the Snow' in *Old Peter's Russian Tales* by Arthur Ransome
- *The Wolf Wilder* by Katherine Rundell

- *Captain Scott's Last Expedition* by Robert Falcon Scott
- *Frankenstein* by Mary Shelley (beginning)

Other titles by Jack London:

- *Call of the Wild*
- *That Spot* (Unit 3 in *Opening Doors to Quality Writing for Ages 10 to 13*)
- *To Build a Fire and Other Favourite Stories*
- *White Fang*

You can find out more on Inuit legends, myths and stories at: www. native-languages.org/inuit-legends.htm.

Wings to fly

We have continuously emphasised choice in terms of writing titles. The exact wording could be negotiated with your pupils if it helps to boost their enthusiasm, but always ensure that new writing territory is explored in a challenging way. Excellence can be pursued by imitating London's carefully plotted journey for the man (and the reader) towards ultimate tragedy.

It makes sense for the children to craft a desolate, frozen scene to exploit the new vocabulary they have learnt from the extracts. Much of the link reading will support the confidence they need to set a tale in the Alaskan past, but we've included other options too. From experience, a focus will help the intensity of the writing – and London has given us all a terrific model.

A planning tip would be to compose a **fortune line** to help your pupils think through the changes in pitch and tone needed in their writing. The graph could be plotted on a large sheet of sugar paper with sticky notes appended to chart each high and low. What have they learnt from London's careful manipulation of our expectations?

❦ Rewrite the end of the 1908 version with the man surviving. How does he do it?

❦ In the 1902 version the traveller survives. Write an account for his friends giving advice on life in Alaska.

❦ Can you recall feeling bitterly cold? If so, write about what happened and how you felt. Were you in danger?

❦ Write a fairy story for younger readers set a long time ago in the frozen wastes.

❦ Write a tense tale, drawing in the reader step by step, just like Jack London does. You could set it in any time or place but your main character needs to endure an ordeal and survive. It could be:

  ❧ An Escape from the Rising Tide

  Or a possibility with a different angle:

  ❧ I Had 24 Hours to Save My Friend

❦ Write a story with a main character who starts off confidently on a journey but, for reasons you need to explain, his or her confidence evaporates!

❦ Rewrite key parts of the 1908 version written in the first person.

❦ A tale of the frozen wastes – in one hundred years' time!

❦ The Snow Fox

❦ The Polar Bear

Don't forget the huge opportunities for dialogic talk when debating these options. Much can be learnt by your pupils from weighing up the challenges and pleasures of the many different angles. To be successful, your pupils will have to build an atmosphere and a fire of anticipation as their audience wonders what will happen!

It's quite possible for young writers to get carried away with fantastical ideas and cumulative, rapid events, so it's worth taking advice from Leo Tolstoy, the author of *War and Peace*: 'Don't spare your labour,' he wrote in 1890, 'write as it comes, at length, and then revise it, and above all shorten it. In the business of writing, gold is only obtained, in my experience, by sifting.' So, let the pen flow first and then edit, revise and cut. Just think how long *War and Peace* might have been!

Unit 10

The Green Door

'The Door in the Wall' by H. G. Wells

Opening Doors key strategy: mind movement

How well can you understand the ways in which H. G. Wells creates a world beyond reality?

Can you effectively create your own world beyond the 'door'?

Access strategies

Start with this sliver of text and the illustration:

Resource 32

Then, he said, he had a gust of emotion. He made a run for it, lest hesitation should grip him again; he went plump with outstretched hand through the green door and let it slam behind him. And so, in a trice, he came into the garden that has haunted all his life.

It was very difficult for Wallace to give me his full sense of that garden into which he came.

There was something in the very air of it that exhilarated, that gave one a sense of lightness and good happening and well-being; there was something in the sight of it that made all its colour clean and perfect and subtly luminous. In the instant of coming into it one was exquisitely glad – as only in rare moments, and when one is young and joyful one can be glad in this world. And everything was beautiful there …

What do your pupils think the narrator will find in the garden? Ask them to make predictions but to base them on the style as well as the content of the text: how Wells expresses the action through the mind of Wallace conditions our expectations. Ask them to come up with questions placed on sticky notes around the illustration.

Most of your pupils should now be ready to write a **taster draft** which is snappy, quick, inventive and ambitious. Limit the words and/ or the timing because this is a learning tool; the sustained and developed writing can come later. Others may need more support first – for example:

- List the vocabulary suggesting that something positive is to come.
- Explore the meanings of words and spellings like 'luminous' and 'exhilarated'.

This will help them to engage with the content and compose a draft which links the positive mind of the narrator with what he encounters.

Use the taster drafts for assessment for learning. Often, the more challenging the writing, the more there is to learn from the feedback.

Teachers in 'Opening Doors' schools are frequently astonished at how readily pupils imitate a great writer and start to push the boundaries of their writing potential. Schools which study challenging texts report much more curiosity and enthusiasm for demanding texts as pupils progress through the school and into Key Stage 3.

The habit of stretching children's minds for comprehension and creativity helps to build resilience. The recurrent use of taster drafts and quality feedback can be the vehicle for more resilience to develop. When learning dialogues are rich, taster drafts are exciting and support language development. However, it is important to bear in mind Shirley Clarke's advice that 'Metacognitive strategies work best when linked with learning contexts, rather than separated. So a lesson on what resilience means is not as effective as discussing resilience in the context of a challenging task for instance' (@shirleyclarke, 3 May 2018).

Writing for reading is also recommended, especially writing about features of the text before responding fully to a sustained piece. Creative writing can enhance understanding because your pupils are crafting ideas from fascinating models. In *Reading Reconsidered*, Doug Lemov et al. (2016: 8) say: 'there are deep synergies between learning to read well and learning to write well'. In your feedback, you will be able to teach them explicitly about the text and they will be listening more intently because they have already experimented with their own writing!

Do enjoy this creative piece inspired by H. G. Wells by a pupil from Ash Grove Academy in Macclesfield:

Stepping through the door, I saw an enchanted garden, rich and verdant, full of the most vibrantly coloured flowers I'd ever seen. Looking up, I notice the sparkle of the sun as it shone through the dancing leaves of the trees that towered over the flowers. Further off, beyond the forest, there was a shimmering lake. I watched as woodland creatures, unafraid, came casually down to the water, making ripples as they drank, which slowly spread outwards across the surface of the water in ever expanding circles. For me, it felt like paradise.

Grace Bailey-Rushton

Bob says ...

Consider what has been learnt from H. G. Wells and a great teacher here! You can build a richer curriculum around quality texts, even when focusing on short passages, because the link reading provides whole-text experiences.

Reading journeys

It's now an easy matter to read the full extract with your class listening intently. Ask them to notice all aspects of the enchanted garden as you read and compare Wells' vision with their own.

Wallace mused before he went on telling me. 'You see,' he said, with the doubtful inflection of a man who pauses at incredible things, 'there were two great panthers there ... Yes, spotted panthers. And I was not afraid. There was a long wide path with marble-edged flower borders on either side, and these two huge velvety beasts were playing there with a ball. One looked up and came towards me, a little curious as it seemed. It came right up to me, rubbed its soft round ear very gently against the small hand I held out and purred. It was, I tell you, an enchanted garden. I know. And the size? Oh! it stretched far and wide, this way and that. I believe there were hills far away. Heaven knows where West Kensington had suddenly got to. And somehow it was just like coming home.

'You know, in the very moment the door swung to behind me, I forgot the road with its fallen chestnut leaves, its cabs and tradesmen's carts, I forgot the sort of gravitational pull back to the discipline and obedience of home, I forgot all hesitations and fear, forgot discretion, forgot all the intimate realities of this life. I became in a moment a very glad and wonder-happy little boy – in another world. It was a world with a different quality, a warmer, more penetrating and mellower light, with a faint clear gladness in its air, and wisps of sun-touched cloud in the blueness of its sky. And before me ran this long wide path, invitingly, with weedless beds on either side, rich with untended flowers, and these two great panthers. I put my little hands fearlessly on their soft fur, and caressed their round ears and the sensitive corners under their ears, and played with them, and it was as though they welcomed me home. There was a keen sense of home-coming in my mind, and when presently a tall, fair girl appeared in the pathway and came to meet me, smiling, and said "Well?" to me, and lifted me and kissed me, and put me down and led me by the hand, there was no amazement, but only an impression of delightful rightness, of being reminded of happy things that had in some strange way been overlooked. There were broad red steps, I remember, that came into view between spikes of delphinium, and up these we went to a great avenue between very old and shady dark trees. All down this avenue, you know, between the red chapped stems, were marble seats of honour and statuary, and very tame and friendly white doves.' ...

He mused for a while. 'Playmates I found there. That was very much to me, because I was a lonely little boy. They played delightful games in a grass-covered court where there was a sundial set about with flowers. And as one played one loved ...

'But – it's odd – there's a gap in my memory. I don't remember the games we played. I never remembered. Afterwards, as a child, I spent long hours trying, even with tears, to recall the form of that happiness. I wanted to play it all over again – in my nursery – by myself. No! All I remember is the happiness and two dear playfellows who were most with me ... Then presently came a sombre dark woman, with a grave, pale face and dreamy eyes, a sombre woman wearing a soft long robe of pale purple, who carried a book, and beckoned and took me aside with her into a gallery above a hall – though my playmates were loth to have me go, and ceased their game and stood watching as I was carried away. "Come back to us!" they cried. "Come back to us soon!" I looked up at her face, but she heeded them not at all. Her face was very gentle and grave. She took me to a seat in the gallery, and I stood beside her, ready to look at her book as she opened it upon her knee. The pages fell open. She pointed, and I looked, marvelling, for in the living pages of that book I saw myself; it was a story about myself, and in it were all the things that had happened to me since ever I was born.'

Thousands of schools are using 'Opening Doors' strategies and they have all learnt more about how to read and understand challenging texts. A common concern amongst teachers is that pupils respond well to questions about the meaning of words in a particular line, but less so when an overall feel for the tone of the passage is required. Children need more practice at accessing meaning both between the lines and on the lines. 'The Door in the Wall' is the kind of unusual type of quality writing that can help to support this process.

A number of English experts have commented on the need for this feel for a whole text, instead of thinking about each sentence, or even each word, as 'living' within its own context. We like this quote from Daniel Willingham in *The Reading Mind*. Writing about how he might forget 90% of the detail from a book, he says: 'You lose the details, but retain the gist. So comprehension includes not only understanding the text moment by moment as you read it, but also the development of some overall sense of what the text is about' (Willingham, 2017: 107).

Bob says ...

Is this text too hard? Remember that this book is aimed at 10- to 13-year-olds. In trials, we have used parts of the passage where appropriate. Younger pupils may need less of the 'vision' initially because there are so many images to comprehend. Some pupils will surprise us, though, and will respond more to the mysterious narration than to a standard plot.

To deepen access and engagement try a **mind movement** activity. Sometimes, writers cleverly devise scenes which link with the protagonist's psychological state. Can we be sure that Wallace is really in this garden? How does his memory of going to the garden as a child link with the way he describes the scenes? By analysing the movements of his mind, your readers can start to grasp any deeper meanings.

Bob says ...

In some lessons I've observed there is lots of spotting of trees but no understanding of the shape of the wood. Strategies like mind movement are designed to encourage pupils to read closely for meaning across the entire passage. In this way, they begin to understand how specific techniques contribute to the wider meaning.

Try some of these **reading journey** strategies to deepen appreciation and exploit the richness of a quality text:

❦ Devise a table comparing what we learn about Wallace's life in West Kensington and his vision through the door. For example:

'intimate realities of this life'	'wonder-happy little boy'
Strict home life	Lightness, beautiful

- ❦ Track Wallace's mind movement using different coloured highlighter pens for (1) his West Kensington mindset and (2) his mindset through the door.

- ❦ How would you describe the tone change in the final paragraph?

- ❦ Construct a **fortune line** showing how Wallace's mind journey goes up and down. This could be done one paragraph at a time. Try it as a graph with the vertical line assessing how positive his mindset is and the horizontal line tracking the five paragraphs.

- ❦ Does the passage raise any philosophical questions? Is escapism in the mind a good thing? How 'real' is Wallace's version of his West Kensington life? Did you find the world through the green door wondrous or sinister?

These tasks can be distributed to pupils according to how well they are progressing: the differentiation should come from the learning. All pupils can access more challenging texts – it's just a question of teachers providing the right support.

Those excelling at this point will be ready for an **evidence spotlight** session to help them engage with the language in more depth. This thinking engine is designed to prompt pupils to weigh up a range of evidence, so that they can move from Willingham's 'gist' to the very specific reasoning behind their interpretations. It enables a more forensic approach, but only after the whole passage has been appreciated and many questions have been asked. To go deeper with your pupils, encourage them to decide what kinds of evidence seem more convincing than others by putting the spotlight on key passages.

Challenging texts invite a variety of methodologies, so you might also consider setting some pupils an open, conceptual question like the one on page 150. They may now have the skills to relish it. Ask the boxed questions in the figure too if they need extra support. This radial layout of learning can help with the distribution of opportunities.

The 'excellent responses' criteria are valuable for both devising effective prompt questions and eliciting the level of rigour you expect from pupils. Use it across your teaching teams and in dialogue with your pupils rather than as an arid collection of bullet points on a board.

Excellent responses will:

Key concept: mind movement – narrative technique

- Discuss the contrast between the 'real' world of West Kensington and the garden.
- Explore some detailed examples of language use – for example, the pattern of phrases connected with the panther, the girl and the garden.
- Explain some of the images of 'home' and what they might mean.
- Identify and explain how the final paragraph is different.

Key concept: image and meaning

- Explore the connotations of, for example, gardens as peaceful or books as knowledge.
- Explain why the panther image is different from the associations with a panther you might expect.

Support:
Where is the evidence for a link between the panther and the girl?

Support:
How exactly is the garden described?

How does H. G. Wells create a distinctive world on the other side of the green door?

Support:
What key images are used to describe the woman with the book?

Greater depth:
What inferences are made about Wallace's childhood? What is your evidence?

Can you compare how you learn about the narrator's feelings with two books from the link reading list – for example, *Boy in the Tower* or *The Turn of the Screw*?

You could attempt to prompt some very advanced work by asking your pupils to consider the multilevelled 'action' taking place here. For example:

1. The narrator is listening to Wallace's story.

2. Wallace is remembering his childhood journey through the door.

3. We can only learn the 'truth' by evaluating Wallace's changing mind shifts.

There is much to learn about narrative technique in 'The Door in the Wall'.

Beyond the limit – link reading

The best way to improve children's skills of inference, deduction and evaluation is to read, read, read! Since the first of the 'Opening Doors' books was published in 2014, we've worked with hundreds of schools directly, and thousands indirectly, on making links between the rich texts used in the class and the ongoing quality reading expected of all pupils. Linking whole-text reading with the core curriculum is making a huge difference in these schools. Quality reading should not get relegated to being a bolt-on 'extra'.

The following suggestions will help you to develop the mind movement theme by providing in-depth reading to support cross-referencing. All these texts have clever narrative techniques from which pupils will learn more about the subtleties of storytelling and how a reader may need to track the psychology of the characters. Where can the reader locate the 'truth'?

- ❦ 'There Will Come Soft Rains' by Ray Bradbury
- ❦ *Where the River Runs Gold* by Sita Brahmachari
- ❦ *Wuthering Heights* by Emily Brontë
- ❦ *Coram Boy* by Jamila Gavin
- ❦ *Boy in the Tower* by Polly Ho-Yen
- ❦ *The Turn of the Screw* by Henry James
- ❦ *The Island at the End of Everything* by Kiran Millwood-Hargrave
- ❦ 'The Giant's Necklace' by Michael Morpurgo
- ❦ *I Capture the Castle* by Dodie Smith
- ❦ *Stone Cold* by Robert Swindells

Wings to fly

The taster drafts can now be developed further. Tips and titles could include:

- ❦ Imagine Wallace finds a different creature in the garden. Continue the vision …
- ❦ Some of the 'living pages' of the book tell the story of the garden and how it came to be. Explore the mysteries of the world beyond the door.
- ❦ What games did Wallace play? What happened which would explain why he can't remember?
- ❦ Create your own world which appears to veer from 'real' to 'virtual'.

- Old Gardens
- Walled Gardens
- Secret Gardens
- Midnight Gardens

Bob says ...

The very best writing should experiment with narrative technique and show a mind movement on the part of the narrator which leaves the reader full of curiosity. Encourage a focus on setting (like the garden) to show how the narrator assesses his or her world. Your young writers can learn from the way H. G. Wells switches between the real and the virtual to devise their own contrasts.

The Torpor of Death

The Haunted Hotel by Wilkie Collins

Opening Doors key strategy: the double echo surprise

How well can you recognise the creation of menace in a room?

Can you devise your own original haunted room?

Wilkie Collins is sometimes credited with writing the first mystery story, *The Woman in White*, and the first detective story, *The Moonstone*. Schools across the UK have produced some astonishing work inspired by Unit 1 in *Opening Doors to Quality Writing for Ages 10 to 13*, which features an extract from *The Woman in White*. We wanted to include more Wilkie Collins in this book to show the potential there is for pupils to be exposed to and enjoy accessible Victorian writers.

The Haunted Hotel is vintage Collins and deserves to be better known. In this novel he delves into the macabre and the Gothic. You may feel that the appearance of the severed head at the end of the extract is more suitable for older pupils; however, the context is so melodramatic that black humour is never far away.

There is actually a more graphic description of the head which has been omitted here but which you may wish to use, as appropriate, according to your age group. You can find it here as part of the full text: http://www.gutenberg.org/ebooks/170.

Bob says ...

When your pupils are encouraged to imitate Collins, a reminder of what is suitable may be necessary. Overt blood and gore is too easy to produce; building tension, in the way Collins does, is much harder.

Access strategies

The following passage provides a very cinematic description of the eccentric scene. At a time well before the cinema, Collins asks his readers to visualise the spooky room. Can your pupils piece together what has happened? Do they need to read some of the link texts first to learn more about the macabre?

As the welcome light diffused itself over the room, she turned from the table and looked towards the other side of the bed.

In the moment when she turned, the chill of a sudden terror gripped her round the heart, as with the clasp of an icy hand.

She was not alone in her room!

There – in the chair at the bedside – there, suddenly revealed under the flow of light from the candle, was the figure of a woman, reclining. Her head lay back over the chair. Her face, turned up to the ceiling, had the eyes closed, as if she was wrapped in a deep sleep.

Ask your pupils to predict the type of story this will be from the style and content. They could write up their ideas as a back cover blurb with a visual plan of the story mapped out on sugar paper. Limit the **taster drafts** to fifty words and suggest that excellent responses must give a flavour of the story and focus on the traditions of melodrama and black humour as much as grisly horror.

For support, here is some of the blurb used for the Vintage Classics edition:

An eminent doctor is visited by a desperate woman with a question: am I evil or insane?

In the darkened bedroom of a mouldering palazzo by the Grand Canal, an English lord sickens and suddenly dies.

How are these little mysteries connected? Spend the night in Room 14 of Venice's finest hotel, and find out the truth – if you dare …[1]

---

1 See https://www.penguin.co.uk/books/111/1111236/the-haunted-hotel/9781784871154.html.

Compare this with the blurb written by a Year 6 pupil from Coastlands Primary School in Pembrokeshire:

A grotesque, horrifying object, hovering in mid-air; a terrifying dream, haunting the mind into madness; an inexplicable intrusion in the dead of night: can Agnes ever break free from this genuine nightmare before she loses all sanity? Or will she be compelled to endure this horrific night-terror forever more?

In this gripping novel about dark secrets, perplexing disappearances and sudden, strange happenings, Wilkie Collins plunges the reader into a world of mystery where even the senses cannot be trusted. Have you enough courage to read on ...?

Madeleine Beal

What a promising writer! Have a go at using book cover blurbs to good effect in your teaching. They can inspire predictions and imitations. Ask your pupils to present their peers with blurbs on their own stories!

The subtitle of *The Haunted Hotel* is *A Mystery of Modern Venice*, which may also stimulate more ideas. Can your pupils invent a suitable subtitle when they write their own ghostly tale later on?

Beyond the limit – link reading

Link reading is always an important part of accessing a challenging text; likewise, more reading becomes part of learning at a greater depth too. In this unit, it might be helpful for pupils to browse through some of these texts to understand the context of a haunted room passage written in 1878.

- *Northanger Abbey* by Jane Austen
- *Jane Eyre* by Charlotte Brontë (Unit 14 in *Opening Doors to Famous Poetry and Prose*)
- *Great Expectations* by Charles Dickens (Unit 8 in *Opening Doors to Famous Poetry and Prose* (descriptions of Satis House and Miss Havisham)
- *Rebecca* by Daphne du Maurier
- *Coraline* by Neil Gaiman
- *The Woman in Black* by Susan Hill
- 'Number 13' by M. R. James
- 'The Fall of the House of Usher' by Edgar Allan Poe

Reading journeys

The combination of the illustration, the exploration of the final paragraph and the back cover blurb task should produce some very specific learning about the tone and style needed to understand the full extract.

The key strategy in this unit is the double echo surprise. This will enable you to teach your pupils how to imitate the way Collins creates a shock – the woman in the chair – but how he also echoes this with the further revelation of the head.

Resource 37

As the welcome light diffused itself over the room, she turned from the table and looked towards the other side of the bed.

In the moment when she turned, the chill of a sudden terror gripped her round the heart, as with the clasp of an icy hand.

She was not alone in her room!

There – in the chair at the bedside – there, suddenly revealed under the flow of light from the candle, was the figure of a woman, reclining. Her head lay back over the chair. Her face, turned up to the ceiling, had the eyes closed, as if she was wrapped in a deep sleep.

The shock of the discovery held Agnes speechless and helpless. Her first conscious action, when she was in some degree mistress of herself again, was to lean over the bed, and to look closer at the woman who had so incomprehensibly stolen into her room in the dead of night. One glance was enough: she started back with a cry of amazement. The person in the chair was no other than the widow of the dead Montbarry – the woman who had warned her that they were to meet again, and that the place might be Venice!

Her courage returned to her, stung into action by the natural sense of indignation which the presence of the Countess provoked.

'Wake up!' she called out. 'How dare you come here? How did you get in? Leave the room – or I will call for help!'

She raised her voice at the last words. It produced no effect. Leaning farther over the bed, she boldly took the Countess by the shoulder and shook her. Not even this effort succeeded in rousing the sleeping woman. She still lay back in the chair, possessed by a torpor like the torpor of death – insensible to sound, insensible to touch. Was she really sleeping? Or had she fainted?

Agnes looked closer at her. She had not fainted. Her breathing was audible, rising and falling in deep heavy gasps. At intervals she ground her teeth savagely. Beads of perspiration stood thickly on her forehead. Her clenched hands rose and fell slowly from time to time on her lap. Was she in the agony of a dream? or was she spiritually conscious of something hidden in the room? …

She raised herself from the crouching position which she had assumed in looking close at the Countess; and, turning towards the other side of the bed, stretched out her hand to the bell. At the same instant, she stopped and looked upward. Her hand fell helplessly at her side. She shuddered, and sank back on the pillow.

What had she seen?

She had seen another intruder in her room.

Midway between her face and the ceiling, there hovered a human head …

Nothing visible, nothing audible, had given her any intelligible warning of its appearance. Silently and suddenly, the head had taken its place above her. No supernatural change had passed over the room, or was perceptible in it now. The dumbly tortured figure in the chair; the broad window opposite the foot of the bed, with the black night beyond it; the candle burning on the table – these and all other objects in the room, remain unaltered. One object more, unutterably horrid, had been added to the rest. That was the only change – no more, no less.

As you read out the full passage, ask your pupils to mark in red every way in which the tension builds. This will need a good deal of individual time in complete silence. Then split the class into **evidence circles** and appoint a chair and a scribe. In seven minutes, each group should complete a list of ways in which the tension builds in the extract.

You could also set them the challenge of highlighting any literary techniques which suggest melodrama or play on the expectations of the Victorian reader. You might consider a **music moment** with melodramatic music playing as the debate rages! Try 'Dies Irae' from Verdi's *Requiem*, Mussorgsky's *St John's Eve on Bald Mountain* or the finale from Mozart's *Don Giovanni*.

Now, set the following question with every expectation that all your learners can attempt it because of the rich learning dialogues they have experienced:

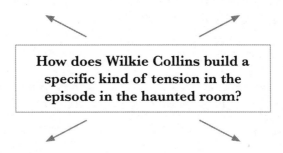

> **How does Wilkie Collins build a specific kind of tension in the episode in the haunted room?**

As with all 'Opening Doors' approaches, support questions can be set. One way of doing this is to base them around the success criteria expectations – for example, a question might be: how is direct speech introduced to good effect?

Excellent responses will:

Key concept: building tension

❧ Discuss the use of light and dark (with examples).

❧ Explore the use of direct speech to create drama.

❧ Identify the importance of the sleeping figure.

❧ Comment on the detail in the description – how short sentences build one after the other.

- Include examples of specific vocabulary which add to the tension, like the 'grinding of teeth'.

- Discuss the double echo effect – the shocking discovery of the woman and the more blatant appearance of the head – and how a summary paragraph links both shocks.

Key concept: building melodrama

- Explore the use of single words, like adjectives – for example, how does 'icy hand' contribute to the melodrama?

- Show how the concept of a haunted room is manipulated by Collins into something new.

- Discuss examples like 'torpor of death', which is a deliberately overplayed phrase.

Feedback should be lively, with ample chance for you to evaluate the pupils' responses and add to their understanding of the text. This might include **intertextuality** links like:

- Finding other passages with the same 'feel' or double echo effect – for example, *Jane Eyre* (Unit 14 in *Opening Doors to Famous Poetry and Prose*) or the passage in *Wuthering Heights* where Lockwood drags Cathy's cold hand across the broken pane!

- Comparing the double echo effect in films or TV adaptations where an initial shock is followed by a second shock. In Hitchcock's famous *Psycho*, the horror of the murder is followed up by the revelation of 'mother' being dead. Recent television drama has taken this further with long series designed for box-set viewing which present twist after twist, such as *Line of Duty*.

- ❦ Linking the ghastliness of the head with comedy or pantomime. Jane Austen's *Northanger Abbey* would provide an interesting comparison of tone.
- ❦ Comparing *The Haunted Hotel* with texts on the link reading list.

Bob says ...

The capacity of pupils to confront the challenge question is dependent on their prior reading. This is why some link reading should be done before the unit is studied. You are training your pupils to expect to read texts which need exploring, questioning and rereading. Top-level comprehension will always come from the most well-read pupils.

Wings to fly

Your pupils might want to develop their thinking on the back cover blurb drafts and write up the full story. Alternatively, there are a range of titles suggested on page 166 which encompass the principle of quality text to quality writing. Encourage your class to imitate Collins, especially the double echo surprise, but they should also put their own ideas into practice too.

You can teach the children about any aspects of writing that you expect to see in their work. It might be using the right adjectives for effect, the ability to be ironic or humorous, the use of prepositional phrases or the chance to focus on spelling patterns, word derivatives or prefix/suffix constructions. Suddenly, spelling, punctuation and grammar work can be fun, relevant and full of questions as your pupils learn how a great writer uses so many tools of the trade!

Do add your own tips and titles to these suggestions:

- ❧ One Hour in a Haunted Room
- ❧ I am the 'Dumbly Tortured Figure in the Chair' and I Have My Story to Tell …
- ❧ Daybreak – the Venetian light from the balcony and a revelation! Explore!
- ❧ Write a melodramatic scene set in a strange hotel.
- ❧ Update the scene to a modern hotel. In what ways will the tension-building be different?

Of course, advice will be needed on using some of the conventions of haunted buildings in entirely new ways – or not at all! This will prevent too many stories of the same type with creaking staircases, wailing banshees and paintings coming to life. The Venetian setting may encourage something new – even Collins is exploiting Victorian melodrama to create an original tone. He is having great fun with the reader, so your pupils might like to try imitating this too!

This is how one Year 6 pupil from Coastlands Primary School practised a double echo surprise within the context of melodrama and black humour:

Annie awoke abruptly from her deep slumber; she opened her casement and scanned the room. Somehow she didn't feel alone. Horrible thoughts still filled her mind – they had been troubling her since her last encounter. Yes! – there! – a dark shadow quickly moved across the wall. What was it? she wondered. As she scrabbled back for her bed she saw it, and an icy hand clasped her pounding heart.

Annie threw herself into her counterpane; her fingernails dug into her hands: she had company in her room.

There – slumped at the most bizarre of angles – there, reclining backwards over Annie's chair, was a woman! Her clothes were soaked in liquids of who knows what; her eyes shut firmly.

'How did you get in here?' Annie cried, her voice crumbling.

Receiving no reply, she slowly crept closer. Annie recognised the figure; every drop of blood in her body was frozen solid; she felt like her own body was conspiring against her. For there – just there – sat no other than old lady Johnson – the very same woman that she had seen in her last troublesome encounter, who had said that they would meet again.

Stirring closer to the lady, Annie clasped the old lady's shoulders and shook her in an effort to wake her – but this was not enough to rouse the sleeping figure. Unsure as to what should be done, she stared towards the other side of the bed chamber. Should she ring for help, or should she go back to sleep (perhaps this was another of those troublesome dreams)? Determining to call for help, she reached for her bell, but instead of grabbing the bell her fingers wrapped around a severed foot!

'What can this mean?' Annie shrieked.

The foot was mildewy and yellow; feeling faint, she ducked into her pillow and hid as her mind was filled with terrible thoughts. What was she to do? Was she ever going to save herself?

Ethan Davies

A Home for David

David Copperfield by Charles Dickens

Opening Doors key strategy: zoom closer

How well can you evaluate the way Dickens helps the reader to visualise the home in a boat?

Can you write about a new kind of home and find original ways to describe it?

Access strategies

It's not surprising that Charles Dickens' works have been filmed so many times – just consider the way young David's view of the landscape goes from the panorama across the beach to the fine detail of the remarkable home within an upturned boat! Dickens manipulates the reader's mind with language in the same way a modern-day film director might with images. A good starting point is to use the illustration or to find stills on the internet from the many films and TV adaptations. If you search under 'Peggotty's boat' you will find some great images from old black and white films and some excellent illustrations from the original book.

Try showing the children a picture of the outside of the boat first, just as David is entering. What do they think he will find inside? The pupils should base their answers on the following paragraph and any links they can make with Dickens or the time in history when *David Copperfield* was written.

Resource 39

I looked in all directions, as far as I could stare over the wilderness, and away at the sea, and away at the river, but no house could *I* make out. There was a black barge, or some other kind of superannuated boat, not far off, high and dry on the ground, with an iron funnel sticking out of it for a chimney and smoking very cosily; but nothing else in the way of a habitation that was visible to *me*.

'That's not it?' said I. 'That ship-looking thing?'

'That's it, Mas'r Davy,' returned Ham.

Use their answers to shape discussions around the likely interior.

Ask the children to write a description of the 'home' inside the boat as a **taster draft** (maximum seventy-five words). Explain that they can imagine it like a freeze-frame and take their minds for a 'walk' around the main room. What would it look like? They should omit people at this stage.

Give advice and credit to those who have begun to zoom in on the detail and relate the objects to a wider atmosphere.

This is how Pranathi Kottamasu from Robin Hood Junior School in Sutton saw the inside of the boat:

However curious and different the exteriors of the house looked like, the inside was akin to any other house someone could live in. The boat was divided into numerous rooms: a living room, bedroom, kitchen and few others. The door led straight into the hall, it was adequate for a family. It has a cosy fireplace in the corner, with coal burning and making everyone warm. Two comfortable chairs sat in the corner, tucked neatly under a small table with a vase of vibrant flowers in the middle. A few paintings hung on the wallpapered walls and added colour to the immaculate and dull house. A corridor leading out of the hall led to a bedroom with a majestic four poster bed in the middle. It had an array of colours in the room, and a small bedside table with fragile ornaments.

The pupils will now enjoy exploring any of the illustrations you found under Peggoty's boat featuring the inside of the boat.

❦ Does the picture match your predictions?

❦ Can you make any connections across the objects?

❦ How would you describe the overall atmosphere of the home?

❦ What kinds of people are you expecting to live there? Why?

Anticipation is a huge weapon in the armoury of great teachers. Your pupils are now so interested that they will demand to see the Dickens passage and will read the descriptions very carefully. You will find that your pupils will listen so much better than if the long extract had been read out at the beginning.

Bob says …

The oracy work involved in exploring the sliver of text and the taster drafts represents an opening up of your pupils' mind to much deeper comprehension possibilities. Encourage them to apply the context of their reading lives and lived experiences to their answers – and then zoom in on the evidence in the text.

Reading journeys

In *David Copperfield*, David goes away with his kind housekeeper, Peggoty. He has not been very happy at home and is captivated by the humble Peggoty household.

Resource 40

I looked in all directions, as far as I could stare over the wilderness, and away at the sea, and away at the river, but no house could *I* make out. There was a black barge, or some other kind of superannuated boat, not far off, high and dry on the ground, with an iron funnel sticking out of it for a chimney and smoking very cosily; but nothing else in the way of a habitation that was visible to *me*.

'That's not it?' said I. 'That ship-looking thing?'

'That's it, Mas'r Davy,' returned Ham.

If it had been Aladdin's palace, roc's egg and all, I suppose I could not have been more charmed with the romantic idea of living in it. There was a delightful door cut in the side, and it was roofed in, and there were little windows in it; but the wonderful charm of it was, that it was a real boat which had no doubt been upon the water hundreds of times, and which had never been intended to be lived in, on dry land. That was the captivation of it to me. If it had ever been meant to be lived in, I might have thought it small, or inconvenient, or lonely; but never having been designed for any such use, it became a perfect abode.

It was beautifully clean inside, and as tidy as possible. There was a table, and a Dutch clock, and a chest of drawers, and on the chest of drawers there was a tea-tray with a painting on it of a lady with a parasol, taking a walk with a military-looking child who was trundling a hoop. The tray was kept from tumbling down by a Bible; and the tray, if it had tumbled down, would have smashed a quantity of cups and saucers and a teapot that were grouped around the book. ... There were some hooks in the beams of the ceiling, the use of which I did not divine then; and some lockers and boxes and conveniences of that sort, which served for seats and eked out the chairs.

All this I saw in the first glance after I crossed the threshold – child-like, according to my theory – and then Peggotty opened a little door and showed me my bedroom. It was the completest and most desirable bedroom ever seen – in the stern of the vessel; with a little window, where the rudder used to go through; a little looking-glass, just the right height for me,

nailed against the wall, and framed with oyster-shells; a little
bed, which there was just room enough to get into; and a
nosegay of seaweed in a blue mug on the table. The walls were
whitewashed as white as milk, and the patchwork counterpane
made my eyes quite ache with its brightness. One thing I
particularly noticed in this delightful house was the smell of
fish; which was so searching, that when I took out my
pocket-handkerchief to wipe my nose, I found it smelt exactly
as if it had wrapped up a lobster. On my imparting this
discovery in confidence to Peggotty, she informed me that her
brother dealt in lobsters, crabs, and crawfish; and I afterwards
found that a heap of these creatures, in a state of wonderful
conglomeration with one another, and never leaving off
pinching whatever they laid hold of, were usually to be found in
a little wooden outhouse where the pots and kettles were kept.

We were welcomed by a very civil woman in a white apron,
whom I had seen curtseying at the door when I was on Ham's
back, about a quarter of a mile off. Likewise by a most
beautiful little girl (or I thought her so) with a necklace of blue
beads on, who wouldn't let me kiss her when I offered to, but
ran away and hid herself. By and by, when we had dined in a
sumptuous manner off boiled dabs, melted butter, and
potatoes, with a chop for me, a hairy man with a very
good-natured face came home. As he called Peggotty 'Lass',
and gave her a hearty smack on the cheek, I had no doubt,
from the general propriety of her conduct, that he was her
brother; and so he turned out—being presently introduced to
me as Mr Peggotty, the master of the house.

'Glad to see you, sir,' said Mr Peggotty. 'You'll find us rough, sir, but you'll find us ready.'

David's view is one of a 'delightful house'. We love the way we are taken into the boat through the eyes of the first-person narrator. Just as David's spirits are lifted, so are ours! It's worth listing the objects carefully and exploring with the children why they seem so special to David – after all, how can a painted tea-tray and a teapot make such an impression? David is enthralled by his room, but why is a nosegay of seaweed so remarkable?

Dickens' descriptions work in a multilayered way, so the radial layout of the questions on page 177 should help you to pitch **reading journeys** appropriately for all your learners.

You may want to use a range of methodologies to help your pupils develop their comprehension skills – the excellence success criteria that follows should help. The dialogues you have in class should be focused on maintaining the appeal of the home in the boat in David's imagination and including some cues as to how Dickens creates this famous scene.

Excellent responses will:

Key concept: first-person narrator

❧ Explain how David's view reflects the images of a home (using examples).

❧ Describe how the punctuation supports David's observations.

Support:
List all the objects inside the boat, including the bedroom. Can you suggest links or connections?

Support:
How is the description of the bedroom linked with David's emotions?
How important is the description of the food?

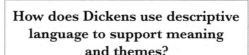

How does Dickens use descriptive language to support meaning and themes?

Support:
Can you write about the overall atmosphere of the main room?
How does the way David sees the objects link with the nature of the Peggotty family? Are they 'rough and ready'?
Why is the way David approaches the boat significant?

Greater depth:
Explore in detail all the ways in which Dickens builds the charm of the home and how David's confidence grows. Is Dickens saying anything about poverty?
Compare and contrast the methods with other passages from Dickens and other sections from *David Copperfield* featuring Mr Murdstone.

❦ Show how David's emotions are linked to what he sees, and why.

Key concept: setting and theme – visualising a specific scene via detailed description

❦ Use increasingly complex examples to show how an overall impression mounts of the scene in the boat.

❦ Include David's response to people and the links between setting and theme.

There are many opportunities for **dialogic talk** and **didactic teaching**, too, to ensure that the children's love and appreciation of this famous episode is cemented. Try preparing your teaching priorities around the following themes:

❦ The sea.

❦ The nature of the home.

❦ Poverty and love.

❦ The romance and charm of the setting through David's eyes – is the smell of fish charming to the reader?

❦ The more distinctive emotions expressed in the bedroom theme.

❦ The way David sees the members of the Peggotty family.

❦ Food! See the food description in *Great Expectations* at Joe Gargery's house (Chapter 4) for comparison.

❦ The repeated linking of objects to meaning and narrative technique.

Beyond the limit – link reading

These texts should enable your pupils to read examples of writers zooming closer to give readers in-depth descriptions but often with a narrator who has a particular mood on how he or she sees it (as in Wallace's description of the garden in Unit 10). Some of them also reflect characters who are searching for a home or an identity.

🐛 *The Phantom Coach* by Amelia Edwards (Unit 2 in *Opening Doors to Quality Writing for Ages 10 to 13*)

🐛 *The Matchbox Diary* by Paul Fleischman

🐛 *Mr Corbett's Ghost* by Leon Garfield

🐛 *Brighton Rock* by Graham Greene (the description at the start of Bank Holiday crowds)

🐛 *The Clay Marble* by Minfong Ho

🐛 *Journey to the River Sea* by Eva Ibbotson (e.g. Chapter 2 – the journey down the Amazon)

🐛 'Through the Tunnel' by Doris Lessing

🐛 *Where the World Ends* by Geraldine McCaughrean

🐛 *The Nowhere Emporium* by Ross MacKenzie

🐛 *The Other Side of Truth* and *Journey to Jo'burg* by Beverley Naidoo

🐛 'I Used to Live Here Once' by Jean Rhys

🐛 *The Little Prince* by Antoine de Saint-Exupéry

🐛 *The Lost Thing* by Shaun Tan

🐛 *Chinese Cinderella* by Adeline Yen Mah

Other books by Charles Dickens:

- *A Christmas Carol*
- *David Copperfield*
- *Great Expectations* (Unit 8 in *Opening Doors to Famous Poetry and Prose*)
- *Little Dorrit*

Wings to fly

The **zoom closer** strategy can be added to the many and varied ways in which your pupils start to comprehend challenging texts. The more styles of writing they can add to their repertoire, the more confident they will become when faced with unseen texts:

> When readers engage with texts, they bring to bear their unique life experiences including their own reading histories. Thus, the sense readers make of a text is more likely to be unique … For this reason, telling readers what to comprehend is of limited value. It is more helpful to give them access to tools that will show them *how* to comprehend. (Tennent et al., 2016: 44)

Bob says …

The whole process of reading literature can be signposted as a lifelong journey of enquiry – a much richer curriculum goal than reading narrowly for test practice.

The children's appreciation of Dickens, as well as the zoom closer strategy, can now be applied to some creative writing. Choose from:

❦ My Attic Bedroom

❦ A Visit to My Eccentric Relation's Home

❦ An Upturned Boat Home in 2120

❦ Virtual Room

❦ Den on the Shore

❦ Describe a different room in the upturned boat.

Short burst taster drafts can be explored on any of these themes initially. They are very visual so illustrations may help. Give advice based on the drafts, with the 'excellent responses will' guidance in mind to elicit improvements. Key questions might be:

❦ How clear and appropriate are your descriptions?

❦ Does the narrator's view link with the descriptions?

❦ Do setting and meaning complement one another?

❦ Is it original?

Here are some examples from pupils at Wicor Primary School in Fareham in response to the theme of rooms, dens and original ways of writing about rooms.

Pushing hard, I pulled myself up an old wooden ladder which creaked with every step and was covered in tons of velvety-green moss. Finally, I reached the top but saw no door, just an old window with rotting wood and broken glass. I squeezed through and found myself in a small damp room, where autumn leaves had made a carpet for me – some flaming red, orange or brown. A small battered mattress lay covered with a bedspread of sycamore keys and an aged blanket, homemade, probably knitted, was curled up waiting. On a table lay porcelain dolls in silken cloth clothing and long ginger ponytails; clearly loved, and hidden in a far corner was a small stove, once busy but now dormant. Next to the stove was a hazel basket filled with the forest's wonders; pine cones, dried berries and more – their scent filled the air. A family of squirrels pattered over the top of this old weathered place with hushed steps.

Walking back over to the window, I stared at the forest surrounding me and at the ladder that got me here.

Alexander Williams

As my foot sunk into the soft sand, the sea started to creep towards me. I trod towards a great hole in the cliff face, circled with shells. My curiosity was piqued, so I went towards it, the sand still clinging onto my bare feet. My hair flowed as the wind kept on pushing. Inside the cave was a velvety throne, I went to sit on the elaborate chair which emitted a royal aura, and which enveloped me. It felt like I was sitting on a queen's throne. It was neatly placed in one of the corners. In another was the most sumptuous, magnificent chest there ever was, masterfully engraved with flowers and swirls. It was full of gems and crystals but on top of all the treasures there was the most extraordinary and detailed shell I had ever seen. It had six eyes of gold. Strips of pink and purple and flecks of silvers all around it. Turning around, there was a yellow and red bucket with a beautiful blue spade sticking out of the top, sitting there like brother and sister. Resting peacefully in a deck chair, just plonked in a random space. Someone had painted the sides of the den like I would my home with patterns of blue for the sea and a beige colour for the sand. Hanging up was a banner advertising the beach when it was first opened for the public. But now it nearly looks the same. The den felt like another home where I could enjoy the beach by myself and savour some alone time. The air inside smelt like damp wood and the salty sea water. I could tell no-one had been here for a long time because there were whittled colouring pencils and plain white paper, discoloured by time.

Lily-Anne Knobel

I (Bob) try to make a writing contribution of my own in all the 'Opening Doors' books. I hope you will enjoy my poetic response to a memory about a beloved home and the day, long ago, when I searched through an old, unopened crate and discovered there was more to my father than I had quite realised. I hope you will find it thought-provoking rather than sad. As I'm always saying to teachers, it's important that we join in with our own writing development too.

The Crate

A crate,
Chiselled and levered:
We opened it.
Thirty years before,
From foreign seas,
It found a home in the old garage,
Secret,
Silent,
Scarred with tape
Like torn bandages.

Loss made me strong.
The creak split my head,
Nails tearing up like studs,
Laid bare now …

Years ago,
The papers of a life:
We opened them.
Strewn like presents
On his lawn:
A medal,
A pewter mug,
Elephants in sepia,

The Temple of the Tooth,
A lost sister in his first garden,
'Whitehall' –
Secret stamps in blue.

The part of our father we never knew.

Urge your pupils to find out more about Dickens. Much of what he wrote was published in magazines; what look like long novels to us were presented in exciting episodes to the Victorian public who waited with bated breath to receive the next instalment. It sounds just like a soap opera!

Dickens left us lots of famous quotes and, like Shakespeare, we are not always aware how they have become embedded in our culture. Try this one from *David Copperfield*: 'My advice is, never do tomorrow what you can do today. Procrastination is the thief of time. Collar him!' Or this one from *A Tale of Two Cities:* 'It was the best of times, it was the worst of times.'

How many more famous Dickens quotes can your pupils find?

Resource 41

Unit 13

A Ghost Mystery for Flaxman Low

'The Story of Baelbrow' by E. and H. Heron

Opening Doors key strategy: sense appeal

How can a ghost story be developed effectively?

Can you chill your reader with apprehension?

E. and H. Heron are the pseudonyms of Major Vernon Hesketh Prichard and his mother Kate O'Brien Ryall Prichard. Together they wrote ghost stories of a macabre type – their main character, Flaxman Low, is a ghost hunter! 'The Story of Baelbrow' was written in 1898.

Access strategies

Show your pupils the first four paragraphs of the extract on pages 191–193 (up until 'he was awaiting for a certain sound').

Try a **sense appeal** role play. In groups of three, one pupil should direct the scene by giving prompts and advice to the second pupil who is Flaxman Low. The third pupil maps out a **fortune line** showing on a graph where in the text the atmosphere becomes tense. Can each group add sound effects?

Now, ask the group to act out Low's movements and give further advice along these lines:

- Are Low's movements the appropriate ones given the anxiety of the situation?
- How do the sounds and sights condition the tension?
- How do the writers use dark and light for effect?

Bob says …

Drama can enhance most of the reading and writing journeys in 'Opening Doors'. This will simultaneously improve the children's drama skills and deepen their understanding of the text. Getting the movement right is a real challenge, so make sure advice for improvement is given and excellent models are appreciated.

Great writers have developed the ghost story genre in numerous ways. It's important to emphasise that suspense, surprise and an appeal to the senses are more important in creating a chill for the reader than overt blood and gore. Before reading the whole extract (or the whole story), try to find some useful parallels in the **link reading** now, rather than later, and transmit some of this knowledge to the children in an enthusiastic way.

Professor of cognitive psychology Daniel Willingham says that 'the ability to read a text and make sense of it is highly correlated with background knowledge. If you know more, you are a better reader' (Willingham, 2006; citing Kosmoski et al., 1990). We have suggested doing this in various ways in the 'Opening Doors' series, and the advantages of integrating the link reading expectations into the core curriculum are plain to see. 'Opening Doors' schools plan for link reading, often based around imaginative themes that reflect our **reading journeys**: tube maps, trees, mountains and even the school itself. What matters is the expectation that children will read quality texts, both in and out of school. An important feature of a richer English curriculum is to read widely, read deeply, read for pleasure, read for fun and read for challenge!

Professor Teresa Cremin has led important research via the United Kingdom Literacy Association and the Open University into the importance of teachers' own reading in facilitating reading for pleasure initiatives. When pupils and teachers read for pleasure, reading communities grow. Many book groups have developed around the country, with teachers who read becoming readers who teach! To find out more visit: www.researchrichpedagogies.org/research.

Bob says ...

Map in key concepts, ambitious objectives and quality texts throughout your school. If you complement this with link reading as a norm, your curriculum design will be enriched. A great teacher adds value to whatever is being read independently by ensuring that the texts used in classrooms go deeper and ask new questions. This is one way for the love of famous stories and poems to take root. If a teacher does not introduce quality texts to pupils, the opportunity may be lost for a lifetime. Reading for challenge is reading for pleasure too.

The more quality reading is part of the reading for pleasure curriculum, the deeper the learning. You could ask your pupils to identify how authors build tension or use the senses for effect in any of the following:

- ❦ 'The Signalman' by Charles Dickens
- ❦ *The Hound of the Baskervilles* by Sir Arthur Conan Doyle (Unit 6 of *Opening Doors to Quality Texts for Ages 10 to 13*)
- ❦ *The Woman in White* by Wilkie Collins (Unit 1 of *Opening Doors to Quality Writing for Ages 10 to 13*)
- ❦ *Dracula* by Bram Stoker (Unit 13 of *Opening Doors to Famous Poetry and Prose*)
- ❦ A chosen extract from the link reading list.

Encourage **intertextuality** by sticking these extracts onto a single sheet of sugar paper and asking the children to identify cross-references to sound, sight, touch, smell or taste. Why do they think this important?

The aim of knowledge acquisition is to build up a bank of understanding that will help your pupils to appreciate the sophistication of the ghost story genre.

Reading journeys

A **taster draft** predicting how Low will encounter the ghost will give your pupils a chance to apply their knowledge and compare their own writing with your reading of the extract. A big debate should then follow on how to improve the use of sense appeal in the drafts and how E. and H. Heron have set up the appearance of the ghost.

Scientist and ghost hunter Flaxman Low has been called to a country house in East Anglia by Professor Van der Voolt. There have been reports of disturbances involving a ghost. The Swaffam family live at the house called Baelbrow and have invited the Van der Voolt family to stay for the summer as Mr Swaffam Senior is away. The professor's daughter is engaged to Harold Swaffam. Ghostly happenings have interrupted the holiday – a maid has been killed and a figure with a bandaged arm has been seen.

Flaxman Low agrees to keep watch at night. A gale is blowing outside.

The early part of the night passed over uneventfully. A light burned faintly in the great wainscotted hall, but the passage was dark. There was nothing to be heard but the wild moan and whistle of the wind coming in from the sea, and the squalls of rain dashing against the windows.

As the hours advanced, Mr Low lit a lantern that lay at hand and, carrying it along the passage, tried the museum door. It yielded, and the wind came muttering through to meet him. He looked round at the shutters and behind the big cases which held Mr Swaffam's treasures, to make sure that the room contained no living occupant but himself.

Suddenly he fancied he heard a scraping noise behind him, and turned round, but discovered nothing to account for it. Finally, he laid the lantern on a bench so that its light should fall through the door into the passage, and returned again to the hall, where he put out his lamp, and then once more took up his station by the closed door of the smoking room.

A long hour passed, during which the wind continued to roar down the wide hall chimney, and the old boards creaked as if furtive footsteps were gathering from every corner of the house. But Flaxman Low heeded none of these; he was awaiting for a certain sound.

After a while, he heard it – the cautious scraping of wood on wood. He leant forward to watch the museum door. *Click, click,* came the curious dog-like tread upon the tiled floor of the museum, till the thing, whatever it was, paused and listened behind the open door. The wind lulled at the moment, and Low listened also, but no further sound was to be heard, only slowly across the broad ray of light falling through the door grew a stealthy shadow.

Again the wind rose, and blew in heavy gusts about the house, till even the flame in the lantern flickered; but when it steadied once more, Flaxman Low saw that the silent form had passed through the door, and was now on the steps outside. He could just make out a dim shadow in the dark angle of the embrasure.

Presently, from the shapeless shadow came a sound Mr Low was not prepared to hear. The thing sniffed the air with the strong, audible inspiration of a bear, or some large animal. At the same moment, carried on the draughts of the hall, a faint, unfamiliar odour reached his nostrils. Lena Van der Voort's words flashed back upon him – this, then, was the creature with the bandaged arm!

Again, as the storm shrieked and shook the windows, a darkness passed across the light. The thing had sprung out from the angle of the door, and Flaxman Low knew that it was making its way towards him through the illusive blackness of the hall. He hesitated for a second; then he opened the smoking-room door that creaked as he opened it.

Harold Swaffam sat up on the sofa, dazed with sleep. 'What has happened? Has it come?'

Ask the children to complete a sense appeal table as a way of identifying the bombardment to the readers' senses of a trail of smells, sights and sounds. The real dread is that there will be a touch!

Sense	Quote	Impact
Auditory	Click, click, came the curious dog-like tread	This is menacing sound. It links with an ongoing tapping and the threat of a beast, but we cannot see it – and nor can Low!
Visual		
Olfactory		

Bob says ...

Teach key concepts in English by getting the pupils to appreciate the whole passage, which can be a common weakness in the teaching of comprehension. There are many ways of doing this, but you could ask the children to identify themes, character traits or techniques as a way of linking paragraphs and appreciating the whole text. If pupils are trained to answer quick questions on specific lines, then that is what they will get used to doing. However, if they are trained to find connections, then harder questions become more accessible. This needs to be embedded throughout all the key stages.

In addition, you could try using a **continuum line** to support the pupils' thinking about the degree of effect of the words or phrases they have identified. This could range from those that add slightly to the atmospheric build-up to those with the greatest effect.

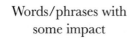

Words/phrases with some impact	Words/phrases with very effective impact

It goes without saying that the dialogues around why selections have been made will be rich, deep and full of debate. You can clarify, advise or add other examples from the link reading texts to go deeper still.

Your pupils can now take on the challenge of the richer 'Opening Doors' question. (See figure on page 196.) Create groups according to progress rather than ability so that all learners share the objectives. The scaffolding takes the form of support questions which you can layer in when needed. Gradually, a 'handover' will occur as the learners take on more responsibility and move on to more challenging questions or greater depth exploration. This is well described in Tennent et al. (2016: 42–43; see also Bruner, 1983).

Excellent responses will:

Key concept: atmosphere and anticipation

- ❦ Demonstrate how the reader senses the approach of the ghost through Flaxman Low's movements and feelings.
- ❦ Show how the use of language, punctuation and grammar contribute to the rising tension.
- ❦ Mention how key dramatic moments, like the reference to the bandaged arm, heighten the tension and create a climax.

Support:
Work out in stages what Low can sense. Look back at your table. Is it more chilling that the ghost is not seen? How important are references to the senses?

Support:
List the words and phrases that refer to the ghost. How are they different? What effect is created? Why is the narrative technique important?

How does the atmosphere build as the ghost comes near?

Support:
How is the action created? Consider fronted adverbials, connectives and sentence length.

Greater depth:
Read any two other approaches to ghosts in different stories. How do the techniques differ? Which is your favourite, and why?

❦ Describe how Low's senses and our own are engaged.

❦ Show how we only get slivers of light and hints of what the ghost looks like.

Of course, your pupils will want to read the full story – you can find it here: http://public-library.uk/ebooks/13/98.pdf.

Beyond the limit – link reading

❦ *Wuthering Heights* by Emily Brontë

❦ *The Haunted Hotel* by Wilkie Collins (Unit 11)

❦ 'The Signalman' by Charles Dickens

❦ *The Hound of the Baskervilles* by Sir Arthur Conan Doyle (Unit 6 in *Opening Doors to Quality Writing for Ages 10 to 13*)

❦ *The Phantom Coach* by Amelia B. Edwards (Unit 2 in *Opening Doors to Quality Writing for Ages 10 to 13*)

❦ *The Graveyard Book* by Neil Gaiman

❦ *The Owl Service* by Alan Garner

❦ *The Woman in Black* by Susan Hill

❦ 'Lost Hearts', 'The Tractate Middoth' and 'The Treasure of Abbot Thomas' by M. R. James

❦ *The Time of the Ghost* by Diana Wynne Jones

❦ *Goth Girl and the Ghost of a Mouse* by Chris Riddell

❦ *Dracula* by Bram Stoker

❦ *Classic Ghost Stories* edited by Vic Parker

❦ *The Young Oxford Book of Ghost Stories* edited by Dennis Pepper

Wings to fly

Try reflecting on what you and your pupils have loved the most about E. and H. Heron's use of the senses. This will help establish the link between quality text and quality writing. I (Bob) love the effect of that lantern light through the passage. What does Low see or not see? The reader shares his limited view and maybe his limited understanding of the threat before him. There is an impression that the ghost hunter has understood the nature of the beast but it's too early for the reader to know. We are kept on the edge of our seats!

Which of these titles give your pupils the best opportunity to show they can use sight, smell, taste, hearing or touch to spooky effect?

❦ An Encounter with the Silent Form

❦ Shades and Shadows

❦ The Museum Door was Half-Open …

❦ The Bandaged Arm

❦ My own Flaxman Low story

❦ An original ghost story to include the following:

  ❧ A night-time setting.

  ❧ Something heard or smelt but never seen.

  ❧ An open ending.

Bob says ...

Your pupils can imitate E. and H. Heron and tell us just enough about the sights and sounds of the ghost to raise questions. The reader should wonder if, or when, some dreadful event may occur. The denouement can be a mixture of a satisfying explanation of events mixed with one or two pulsating sentences which give a sense of the unknown.

In the full version of 'The Story of Baelbrow', I enjoyed this section towards the end:

Resource 42b

Half in and half out of an oblong wooden box in a corner of the great room, lay a lean shape in its rotten yellow bandages, the scraggy neck surmounted by a mop of frizzled hair. The toe strap of a sandal and a portion of the right foot had been shot away.

Swaffam, with a working face, gazed down at it, then seizing it by its tearing bandages, he flung it into the box, where it fell into a lifelike posture, its wide, moist-lipped mouth gaping up at them.

It is Swaffam's reaction that I enjoy: savage, angry and swift! This moment comes after building tension, many uncertainties and the threat of death. It's very easy to write a ghost story which descends into silliness and stereotyping; it's very challenging to write one with some of the ingredients we expect but with a genuine chill! Encourage your pupils to focus on the senses as a way of imitating this successfully.

Shame and Pain

Little Women by Louisa May Alcott

Opening Doors key strategy: taut tension

To what extent can you understand the way tension builds in a narrative?

Can you develop your own dramatic tension in an episode or story?

Access strategies

Offer the short extract on page 202 first and ask your pupils to debate when the story may have been written. What evidence do they have of any kind of time frame? Don't tell them about *Little Women* or provide any background to the text. Let them explore. They might like to apply a popular 'Opening Doors' **thinking engine** known as **noticed, noted, not sure** in table form:

Noticed	Noted	Not sure

The pupils can discuss in groups what they notice that initially puzzles or interests them, what one thing they would each note down as being most important, and what questions they need to ask about vocabulary or meaning. This is a good habit to introduce as regular classroom practice.

Bob says ...

If there is nothing to put in the 'not sure' column, then the text you are using is not challenging enough!

It was a most unfortunate moment for denouncing Amy, and Jenny knew it. Mr Davis had evidently taken his coffee too strong that morning; there was an east wind, which always affected his neuralgia; and his pupils had not done him the credit which he felt he deserved: therefore, to use the expressive if not elegant language of a schoolgirl, 'he was as nervous as a witch, and as cross as a bear'. The word 'limes' was like fire to powder; his yellow face flushed, and he rapped on his desk with an energy which made Jenny skip to her seat with unusual rapidity.

'Young ladies, attention, if you please!'

At the stern order the buzz ceased, and fifty pairs of blue, black, grey and brown eyes were obediently fixed upon his awful countenance.

'Miss March, come to the desk.'

The reader can only understand how the tension builds by appreciating the exact inferences which add up to make an overall 'feel' of threat to Amy. To lay the foundations of learning how Louisa May Alcott builds tension, ask the class to find every description or inference connected with the teacher's personality. Can they build a profile and, by doing so, predict what may happen? For example:

❦ What is inferred by the coffee and the east wind?

❦ What are limes? Why might they be important?

❦ Why is his physical look important? What is neuralgia?

This exercise will provide high-level practice on how meaning is linked with association and our prior reading and general knowledge. It is classroom dialogue that will stitch together the map of learning and draw out pupils' memories and deductions. Unfamiliar vocabulary can be explained with the help of examples.

A **taster draft** will give your pupils an opportunity to experiment with new words: ask them for a paragraph describing someone who is nervous. It doesn't have to be set at school. Keep the focus on one person only. Potential scenarios could be:

❦ At a bus stop.

❦ At a sports event.

❦ At an airport or railway station.

Borrow some of the **zoom closer** strategies from the *David Copperfield* passage in Unit 12 to encourage the children to think deeply about someone on edge.

Bob says ...

Challenging texts, including ones with archaic language, offer the greatest opportunities for learning because there is so much to explore.

'Opening Doors' units are designed to be accessed by all learners, so it has been inspirational to see so many learners who have previously missed out on high-level programmes being able to enjoy great literature and improve their basic skills as a consequence of their ownership of the texts. Martin Stephen and Ian Warwick (the director of London Gifted & Talented) (2015: 133) list the following features which tend to arise with pupils who are classed as 'high potential' but are at risk of underachievement:

- They have 'more gaps in their academic vocabulary'.

- They take things 'more literally than intended'.

- They 'lack cultural capital'.

- They haven't been exposed to 'the diversity of history and society critical to achievement'.

- They are less likely to be familiar with 'the conventions and expectations of academic writing'.

Schools that have utilised 'Opening Doors' resources – and, of course, adapted them for their own context – have found that the study of challenging texts through Key Stages 1, 2 and 3 has raised aspirations. Certainly, literature is an equal opportunities issue: the sooner it is encountered, the sooner confidence can grow – as long as the access strategies are in place to open doors.

Reading journeys

Your pupils will now be able to make knowledgeable predictions about what may happen to Amy and how the tension will continue to build. An interesting question may be to ask them when they think the text was written (approximately) as this will call on their contextual understanding.

Little Women (1868/69) is one of the most famous American novels, and Alcott's portrayal of the March family (based on her own home in Concord, Massachusetts) has become enduringly popular. All literature is greatly enhanced when we have an appreciation of the context in which it was written, but the character of Jo March – with her desire for a career – is often cited as a new direction for female characters.

You can now read the full extract to your expectant class. We love the mix of narrative and direct speech – and remember, Amy is only 12. Our heart sinks with hers as the inevitability of the punishment is interspersed with the clever cameo of the teacher.

Amy March has taken some pickled limes into school. However, sucking them has become such a craze that the teacher, Mr Davis, has banned them. Amy owes limes to other girls and is planning to pay them back. However, a rival pupil, Jenny Snow, gives away the presence of her limes and Amy must face the consequences.

It was a most unfortunate moment for denouncing Amy, and Jenny knew it. Mr Davis had evidently taken his coffee too strong that morning; there was an east wind, which always affected his neuralgia; and his pupils had not done him the credit which he felt he deserved: therefore, to use the expressive if not elegant language of a schoolgirl, 'he was as nervous as a witch, and as cross as a bear'. The word 'limes' was like fire to powder; his yellow face flushed, and he rapped on his desk with an energy which made Jenny skip to her seat with unusual rapidity.

'Young ladies, attention, if you please!'

At the stern order the buzz ceased, and fifty pairs of blue, black, grey and brown eyes were obediently fixed upon his awful countenance.

'Miss March, come to the desk.'

Amy rose to comply with outward composure, but a secret fear oppressed her, for the limes weighed upon her conscience.

'Bring with you the limes you have in your desk,' was the unexpected command which arrested her before she got out of her seat. …

(Mr Davis insists that Amy throws the limes out of the window two by two!)

As Amy returned from her last trip, Mr Davis gave a portentous 'Hem!' and said, in his most impressive manner – 'Young ladies, you remember what I said to you a week ago. I am sorry this has happened; but I never allow my rules to be infringed, and I *never* break my word. Miss March hold out your hand.'

Amy started and put both hands behind her, turning on him an imploring look which pleaded for her better than the words she could not utter. She was rather a favourite with 'old Davis', as, of course, he was called, and it's my private belief that he *would* have broken his word if the indignation of one irrepressible young lady had not found vent in a hiss. That hiss, faint as it was, irritated the irascible gentleman, and sealed the culprit's fate.

'Your hand Miss March!' was the only answer her mute appeal received; and, too proud to cry or beseech, Amy set her teeth, threw back her head defiantly, and bore without flinching several tingling blows on her little palm. They were neither many nor heavy, but that made no difference to her. For the first time in her life she had been struck; and the disgrace, in her eyes, was as deep as if he had knocked her down.

At this point, you can link the illustration with other famous images on the theme of the Victorian schoolroom and attitudes to punishment – search for 'Squeers' in *Nicholas Nickleby* or 'Lowood' in *Jane Eyre*. How do your pupils feel about corporal punishment? Why do they think Amy feels 'disgraced'?

You can now set off on another exciting 'Opening Doors' question which will give opportunities for depth, mastery and new learning at each stage, with every pupil sharing in the journey.

Support:
How do we learn about Mr Davis and why does this matter?
What does 'irascible' mean and why is it an important adjective?

Support:
How does the short paragraph and direct speech contribute to the tension?
Why is the hiss significant?

How does Louisa May Alcott build dramatic tension in the text?

Support:
Track Amy's changing feelings. How does the author help the reader to relate to Amy?

Greater depth:
Compare the way tension is built in *Little Women* with another scene featuring classroom tension (e.g. the village school in *Cider with Rosie* or Dotheboys Hall in *Nicholas Nickleby*). How are the scenes similar or different?

Excellent responses will:

Key concept: how to build tension

❦ Explore the nervous state of a key character, Mr Davis – similes, habits, state of mind, physical details and so on.

❦ Discuss the use of direct speech in contributing to the narrative.

❦ Describe how the feelings of the main protagonist are closely followed by an emotionally involved narrator.

❦ Understand how the uncertainty about Amy's fate is created.

❦ Mention how the reader's sympathies are with Amy as she 'defiantly' accepts the punishment.

Beyond the limit – link reading

The following titles are focused on the theme of the classroom. As always, there is a variety of challenge because, whatever their age, children will be at vastly different points in their development. You may wish to introduce these texts for comparative purposes at an appropriate point.

❦ *Rebound* by Kwame Alexander

❦ *To Sir, With Love* by E. R. Braithwaite

❦ *The Chocolate War* by Robert Cormier

❦ *The Demon Headmaster* by Gillian Cross

❦ *Matilda* by Roald Dahl

- ❦ *Nicholas Nickleby* by Charles Dickens (see Wackford Squeers)
- ❦ *Oliver Twist* by Charles Dickens (see Mr Bumble)
- ❦ *Kes* by Barrie Hines
- ❦ *Cider with Rosie* by Laurie Lee (see the village school)
- ❦ *Picnic at Hanging Rock* by Joan Lindsay
- ❦ 'Harry Potter' series by J. K. Rowling
- ❦ *Holes* by Louis Sachar
- ❦ *The Prime of Miss Jean Brodie* by Muriel Spark
- ❦ *Roll of Thunder, Hear My Cry* by Mildred D. Taylor

Other books by Louisa May Alcott:

- ❦ *Good Wives*
- ❦ *The Inheritance*
- ❦ *Jo's Boys*
- ❦ *Little Men*

Wings to fly

The **key concept** of creating taut tension can be applied in many different contexts, but try to reflect on the 'excellent responses' criteria which are intended to guide teaching teams and jumpstart learning dialogues. What has been learnt from Louisa May Alcott can now be applied to achieve quality writing.

Try one or more of these suggestions:

- Write Jenny Snow's version of events in the style of Louisa May Alcott.

- After this event Mr Davis makes Amy stand in front of the class. What happens next?

- Write a passage about your worst day at school with the tension building ...

- Pickled limes were banned in the story but the pupils still kept sucking them! Use the internet to research any of the following items which have been banned from schools, and write a dramatic story about it:
  - Bubble gum
  - Clackers
  - Fidget spinners
  - Light-up Yo-Yos
  - Tamagotchis

- Write a version of events from the viewpoint of one of Amy's friends.

- You tell a lie to avoid the anger of a teacher. How does it happen and why?

- Write about any confrontation at school exploring the feelings of both teacher and pupil.

The school setting may be familiar to your pupils, but it's challenging to create tension – rather than write something flippant or stereotyped – so you may need to warn them about aiming for quality by focusing on the atmosphere, not overt sensation!

Unit 15

Fake News

In Search of the Truth

Opening Doors key strategy: bluff detector

Can you read critically in order to question reliability?

Can you ever write about the 'truth'?

What is the truth? As teachers, we are often faced with tall tales from which we have to unpick who, how and what occurred in the play-ground, dinner hall or corridor. Considering what the truth is, and why people don't always tell the truth, is a skill all children need to develop. We require them to demonstrate it every time we ask them to do research in any curriculum area.

Access strategies

Playing games can get children engaged and ready to learn, and 'truth or bluff' is always a popular choice. Provide groups with three unusual words: give them the definition for one word and ask them to make up a definition for the other two words. Now ask each group to present their words and definitions to the class and get the other pupils to guess the correct word and definition combination. The children will quickly come to realise that they are more likely to believe definitions that are detailed, convincing and delivered with authority – and perhaps hide untruths behind aspects of the truth.

Having looked at successful strategies that can be used to bluff an audience, draw attention to the importance of recording major events. You could refer to current news stories or those that have made a recent impression.

Now consider the Battle of the Somme. Some of the men who fought included Anne Frank's father Otto Frank, Adolf Hitler, Wilfred Owen and J. R. R. Tolkien. Now regarded as one of the bloodiest battles in the history of the British Army, news reports at the time of the battle didn't quite equal the reality of those experiencing it at the Front.

Share some statistics with the children about the Battle of the Somme:

- Lasted 141 days (1 July–18 November 1916).
- The British Army lost 800 aircraft and 252 aircrew were killed.
- 292 tons of bombs were dropped.
- There were 419,654 British casualties.
- On the first day 57,000 British soldiers were injured – in contrast to 185 Germans.
- On the first day 19,240 British soldiers died.
- 90% of Allied casualties were caused by German machine gun.

Ask your pupils to imagine what it might have been like to be present at the first day of the battle. With the children, collect and write down all of the words and phrases that describe how a soldier may have felt, what they would have seen, smelt and tasted. Perhaps the children could create a word cloud in the shape of a bomb using a free online word cloud generator. You could order these in a **continuum line** from least to most affecting and consider why the choice of vocabulary is effective.

You may want to play some music to set the scene during these activities. Consider your **music moment** choice carefully: Gustav Holst's rousing 'Mars, the Bringer of War' from *The Planets Suite* may produce a completely different response than the more melancholic tones of Elgar's 'Nimrod' from the *Enigma Variations* or Paul Hillier's recording of Arvo Pärt's *De Profundis*.

A **taster draft** now will enable the pupils to create their own news account based on facts from the Battle of the Somme. What is the headline? What would the first paragraph include? Encourage the development of ideas from the word bomb, combined with the facts they have gathered.

Having written their own front pages, reveal the headlines from the *Daily Mirror* on 31 July 1916:

❦ 'The General Situation is Favourable'

❦ 'Furious Fighting During the Night'

❦ 'British Capture 3,500 Prisoners'

❦ 'Mightiest Battle of British Army'

For more detail about these headlines take a look at the BBC's website: http://www.bbc.co.uk/history/worldwars/wwone/mirror04_01.shtml.

You can also show pupils the front cover of the *Sunday Pictorial* from 2 July 1916, which can be found at: https://www.bbc.co.uk/news/uk-england-36149839.

The front page images show what seem to be happy British soldiers. Do the children think the soldiers were really happy? How do the facts about the Somme contrast with the headlines and images? Why might the events have been reported in such a positive way?

Now would be a good time to introduce the term 'propaganda'.

It might be helpful to create a table of antonyms to consider how language is used to tell a different or partial story. This will be useful vocabulary to use throughout the unit. You can draw on work from the earlier word bomb.

victorious	defeated
advance	retreat
deaths	survivors
discouraged	heartened

It's now time to read, uncover and rethink how truth has been used in the past. Introduce the pupils to one of the first recorded uses of 'fake news'.

Verity says ...

As readers, we increasingly have to learn how to respond to mass media and news reporting strategies, especially when phrases such as 'the end of truth' and 'post-truth' are becoming more common. Understanding how and why we need to be critical readers is essential in order to decide on the reliability of primary and secondary sources of evidence.

On 2 September 1914, twenty-five leading British authors were invited to a top-secret meeting at the headquarters of the War Propaganda Bureau. Here they discussed ways of best promoting Britain's interests during the war. Those who attended the meeting included Sir Arthur Conan Doyle, Thomas Hardy, Rudyard Kipling, A. A. Milne and H. G. Wells. The aim of the group was to generate positive stories about the Allies and negative stories about the enemy. It proved very successful, and by 1916 the Bureau was printing leaflets about how the Germans were, supposedly, collecting dead bodies from the battlefields, taking them to a 'corpse factory' and boiling them up to make soap. This atrocity was published in a Shanghai newspaper and ignited outrage which resulted in the Chinese declaring war on Germany in 1917. Since the end of the war, evidence has been found that the 'corpse factory' was a fiction.

Read this extract from *The Times* (dated 17 April 1917):

We have known for long that the Germans stripped their dead behind the firing line, fastened them into bundles of three or four bodies with iron wire, and then dispatched these grisly bundles to the rear. ...

the chief factory of which has been constructed 1,000 yards from the railway connecting St. Vith, near the Belgian frontier, with Gerolstein, in the lonely, little-frequented Eifel district, south-west of Coblentz. The factory deals specially with the dead from the West Front. If the results are as good as the company hopes, another will be established to deal with corpses on the East Front. ...

The trains arrive full of bare bodies, which are unloaded by the workers who live at the works. The men wear oilskin overalls and masks with mica eyepieces. They are equipped with long hooked poles, and push the bundles of bodies to an endless chain, which picks them with big hooks, attached at intervals of 2ft.

The bodies are transported on this endless chain into a long narrow compartment, where they pass through a bath which disinfects them. They then go through a drying chamber, and finally are automatically carried into a digester or great cauldron, in which they are dropped by an apparatus which detaches them from the chain. In the digester they remain for six to eight hours, and are treated by steam, which breaks them up while they are slowly stirred by machinery.

A challenging theme, which demands the reader to carefully consider the consequences of the text, is a great way of forging a route to mastery. Ask your pupils the following 'Opening Doors' question. As always, plan from the top and use your questioning skills to develop teaching points. If the children need some help, then guide them using the support questions:

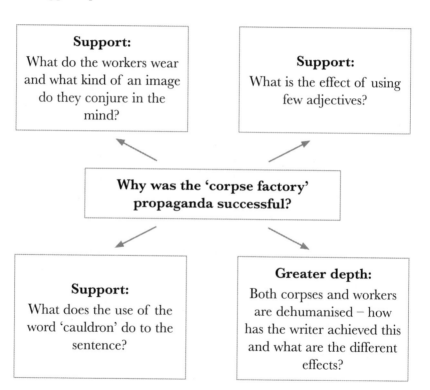

Support:
What do the workers wear and what kind of an image do they conjure in the mind?

Support:
What is the effect of using few adjectives?

Why was the 'corpse factory' propaganda successful?

Support:
What does the use of the word 'cauldron' do to the sentence?

Greater depth:
Both corpses and workers are dehumanised – how has the writer achieved this and what are the different effects?

Excellent responses will:

Key concept: creating an emotive response

❦ Explain how a sense of disgust is created.

❦ Show why the use of the word 'machinery' is so effective in the last sentence.

❦ Understand how the bodies have been dehumanised.

❦ Describe the detailed steps of the procedure.

❦ Show how details about the workers' uniforms and tools develop fear: why would they want to live at the factory? Are they men or monsters?

For more information about the 'corpse factory' article see the BBC's report at: https://www.bbc.co.uk/news/entertainment-arts-38995205.

Beyond the limit – link reading

You can now introduce a mixture of fiction and non-fiction texts in order to get your pupils to question critically what is fact and what is fake. Why have these authors used the strategies they have and what is the effect?

❦ *The Wolf's Story: What Really Happened to Little Red Riding Hood* by Toby Forward – consider the different perspective offered.

❦ *The Land of Neverbelieve* by Norman Messenger – read the opening note from the author and unpick the strategies he has used in order to create a real yet unreal place.

❦ *The True Story of the Three Little Pigs* by Jon Scieszka – compare this with the traditional version of the tale.

❦ *Unwind* by Neal Shusterman – discuss how the author uses real and fictional headlines and news articles to provide the backstory for this dystopia.

❦ *The Arrival* by Shaun Tan – based on the real experiences of immigrants to the United States in the 1800s. Consider how these events have been interpreted in the picture book: what aspects have been explored? You can learn more about this movement of people at: https://www.ducksters.com/history/us_1800s/ellis_island.php.

❦ *The Invisible Man* by H. G. Wells – consider the scientific explanation as to how the 'invisible man' created his fictional invisibility. Could it be true?

❦ *The Diary of a Young Girl* by Anne Frank – this could be compared with fiction works such as *Carrie's War* by Nina Bawden, *Goodnight Mister Tom* by Michelle Magorian or *The Boy in the Striped Pyjamas* by John Boyne. It could also be compared with other non-fiction texts, such as the contemporary narrative *I Am Malala* by Malala Yousafzai or Nelson Mandela's *Long Walk to Freedom*.

The children could also read the news, check out headlines and search for misleading stories. This type of reading can become part of all sorts of cross-curricular enquiry where the mass media, political groups or private companies *may* have influenced stories with a biased perspective – for example: whether seatbelts are safe (personal and social education (PSE)), whether women should have been given the vote (PSE, history), whether the moon landings were faked (history), whether global climate change is happening (geography, PSE, education for sustainable development and global citizenship (ESDGC)) or whether cigarettes and/or vaping is good for you (history, PSE).

Critical reading should raise lots of questions about why and how we write what we write. This isn't a new question. Your pupils may be surprised to learn that Niccolò Machiavelli (1469–1527) was writing about this over 500 years ago: 'Occasionally words must serve to veil the facts. But let this happen in such a way that no one become aware of it; or, if it should be noticed, excuses must be at hand to be produced immediately.'

All of this discussion will begin to unpack the politics of writing and how we, as readers, need to be aware of the writer's purpose. You may want to encourage your pupils to take a more critical view of exactly what it is they are being taught, and why. This short extract from Bertrand Russell's 1922 lecture 'Free Thought and Official Propaganda' provides plenty of food for thought and always gets pupils talking!

Our system of education turns young people out of the schools able to read, but for the most part unable to weigh evidence or to form an independent opinion. They are then assailed, throughout the rest of their lives, by statements designed to make them believe all sorts of absurd propositions, such as that Blank's pills cure all ills, that Spitzbergen is warm and fertile, and that Germans eat corpses. …

Resource 48

If there is to be toleration in the world, one of the things taught in schools must be the habit of weighing evidence, and the practice of not giving full assent to propositions which there is no reason to believe true. For example, the art of reading the newspapers should be taught. The schoolmaster should select some incident which happened a good many years ago, and roused political passions in its day. He should then read to the school children what was said by the newspapers on one side, what was said by those on the other, and some impartial account of what really happened. He should show how, from the biased account of either side, a practised reader could infer what really happened, and he should make them understand that everything in newspapers is more or less untrue. The cynical scepticism which would result from this teaching would make the children in later life immune from those appeals to idealism by which decent people are induced to further the schemes of scoundrels.

Wings to fly

Look back to the taster drafts. The pupils can now apply their new awareness of the purpose of writing and the ways in which the reader can be manipulated. A few ideas that could be followed up include:

- Provide children with a photograph or unusual artefact and discuss possible positive and negative interpretations of it. Set up a class 'write-off', with some pupils writing articles for one interpretation and the rest writing an opposing one. Discuss which writers have used the strategies in this unit most effectively.

❧ Invite the children to invent a fake news story about their school – remember, it needs to be believable!

❧ Ask the children to find out more about the 'corpse factory'. You could use hot seating and interview the children as the 'workers'. After this activity they could create further propaganda material to assist the Allies.

❧ Focus the children's attention on crafting a headline with a specific verb or adjective (set a word limit to ensure punchy, hard-hitting examples).

Alternatively, the children could develop some related non-fiction texts and oracy experiences. Here are some possible projects:

❧ Writing and filming a news broadcast of fake/real news.

❧ Writing instructions on how to create fake news *or* how to ensure you are a critical reader.

❧ Propaganda is communicated through adverts – can your pupils take an advertising campaign and subvert it? This could involve making a poster, designing a website or creating a short TV-style advert that tells an alternative truth – for example, the real stories behind the clothes we buy from the point of view of the garment workers who make them. This alternative story is not told when we see the smiling faces and pristine clothing in catalogues and adverts. See the work of Fashion Revolution for ideas and educational resources: www.fashionrevolution.org.

Glossary

Box planning

This is a very simple idea of presenting stages to pupils in the form of boxes to help them visualise the process and split it into steps. The boxes could become cards, of course!

Context search

This is when various vocabulary exercises may be applied to support an understanding of the context of a word in addition to its dictionary definition.

Continuum line

Once you have set two ends of a continuum, the pupils can decide which words or ideas belong at which position along the line. Discourage rapid decision-making based on 'right' or 'wrong' and instead encourage reflection and the weighing of ideas using evidence. You might say to your pupils, 'To what extent do you think …?' You could first debate a position as a class and then ask the children to stand along a continuum line at the front of the classroom. Explore the issue or idea further and then see who has adjusted their position.

Counterpoint

This is when a writer flags up contrasting moments, feelings or places, although they may be part of the same coherent theme.

Cueing in context

Knowing about a writer's life, the cultural and historical context in which they were writing, and how words might have changed their meaning over time can undoubtedly deepen a reader's personal and critical response to a text. It can also, however, get in the way at times if context is introduced too soon. (See Unit 5 for an example of how a personal connection to, and interpretation of, a metaphor can be nurtured without context and then deepened with a timely cue.)

Deep objective

We refer to this as a way of signalling the need for an objective which genuinely sets up depth and challenge. We usually phrase this as a question.

Dialogic talk

In a dialogic classroom, the teacher and pupils work on the belief that knowledge and understanding are built through discourse. Teachers cannot assume that learners have the necessary oracy skills to explore ideas purposefully together through talk, but they can build such skills with their learners over time through practice and reflection. For more information see: https://www.educ.cam.ac.uk/research/groups/cedir/ or https://www.robinalexander.org.uk/dialogic-teaching/.

Didactic teaching

This phrase has been used for a long time to suggest teacher instruction. On those occasions when new knowledge needs to be explained and pupils guided very definitely, a didactic method can be employed with success. Outstanding teachers know how to adapt their style and choose the right methodology for the right objective.

Direct transmission

Teaching as transmission is the act of transferring facts and concepts from teacher to pupil. The new learning then has to be replicated in some way to 'prove' that the new body of knowledge has been understood and stored in the memory. Direct transmission can be useful in short bursts when you need to explain something in detail, particularly if it needs to be modelled.

Evidence circles

Your classroom can become a place where reasons must always be found for views and opinions. You can then bring the reasons into an evidence circle for discussion.

Evidence spotlight

After all sorts of evidence has been collected to answer a rich, conceptual question, put the spotlight on the most convincing reason.

Excellent responses will (include)

This is a suggested way of ensuring that the most ambitious criteria for success are presented up front. It supports classroom discussions about how the most ambitious challenges can be achieved.

Extended metaphor

This is when a writer adopts a central analogy or conceit and explores various facets and implications in a poem or story.

Fortune line

A fortune line provides a way of tracking the changing emotions of a character, or perhaps a developing atmosphere, through an extract or story. The graph (with time marked along the horizontal axis and whatever you are tracking on the vertical axis) supports pupils to read more carefully, compare their findings with others and go deeper into examples.

Free verse

A tradition of poetry writing that does not have a rhyme scheme or regular rhythm.

Iambic rhythm

The most dominant rhythm in English verse is based on the iamb – the heartbeat rhythm 'de-dum de-dum'. All of Shakespeare's verse plays on setting up the expectation of five iambic feet – iambic pentameter – and then riffing on this 'base' metre, with disruption signalling changes in mood and meaning.

Inform and infer

Develop the habit in your classroom of sifting out the facts from the meaning between the lines. Explore what seems to be information compared with what is being inferred. It's a very helpful access strategy and your pupils can start to apply this method to any unseen text.

Intertextuality

The relationships between literary texts, perhaps based on themes, imagery, style or characters.

Key concepts

One way of designing a richer English curriculum is to map out key concepts for each objective to ensure continuity and progression year by year. This tends to support challenging thinking for all because a concept must be mastered, and the chosen text provides the means to explore the objectives fully. The resulting knowledge and skills can then be applied in more challenging contexts.

Link reading

Try to cross-reference books and poems that you expect your pupils to read. This prevents wider reading from being regarded as an optional or discrete part of the curriculum. Ensure that link reading is mapped in as part of continuity and progression.

Mark and note

A way of retaining the relationship a pupil develops with the text by marking parts of speech or noticeable features, but with more emphasis on asking questions about them. Pupils should explain why they have highlighted certain passages of text and share their views. This also gives the teacher a chance to intervene and clarify any learning points.

Mind link strategy

Any strategy that enables pupils to read a text and find patterns. These themes or patterns will vary from text to text. A table or visual may help to support the linking processes being made in the mind.

Mind movement

This strategy can be used to engage with any text where the narrative viewpoint is complex. More exposure to such texts will gradually start to stimulate more experimentation in writing. Your pupils need to explore ways in which the mind of the narrator can shift in time or where there are multiple narrators.

Mini-plenary

These are feedback sessions with huge opportunities for learning. There should be the chance to share, question and explore progress. You can also teach explicit aspects of spelling, punctuation and grammar in context. Deeper learning and improved outcomes can then follow. Suggested questions might be: what have you found hard? What has interested you the most? How can you improve your writing? What progress have you made?

Morphology

The linguistic study of how words are formed.

Music moments

These are advised throughout the 'Opening Doors' series and are about much more than background music. Music moments can act like the soundtrack to a film – reinforcing meaning and supporting poetry or prose as a performance.

Noticed, noted, not sure

This is a lively thinking sequence to encourage independence, observation and questioning. Pupils can read any kind of text – visual, media or literary – and respond in three ways:

1. Devise a long list of noticed puzzlements in the text.

2. Note down the most important techniques or questions.

3. Include in a third column any other questions.

There should always be words, stylistic points or unusual content about which even the most able are sure about. This will set up your explicit teaching points.

Radial questions

Instead of setting out questions in a traditional linear way, why not offer possibilities radiating outwards from a central, high level question? This gives you the chance to personalise support and introduce new challenges as appropriate. It is a flexible strategy and encourages the pupils to focus on the quality answers needed.

Reading journey

Instead of using the term 'comprehension', why not talk about reading journeys? Emphasise that active and independent approaches to reading make understanding harder texts exciting and full of enquiry – a reading journey for life!

Sense appeal

This is any strategy, including role play, where there is a focus on what is seen, heard, touched or even smelt in a text. This can be a route into exploring the meaning of the text.

Symbolism

In literature, writers often use objects, ideas, events or characters to represent wider meanings so that the overall meaning may be more profound and more ambiguous than the literal meaning.

Symbol source

This is a strategy to encourage links, associations and deeper meaning by exploring a symbol in more detail.

Taster draft

The access strategies should include an early chance to write. This kind of draft should be enriching, not laborious. Your young writers can experiment with style and get advice from you at the point of the most intense enjoyment and deepest learning. The taster draft is a powerful learning vehicle for the improved full version they will write later on.

Thinking engine

A generic phrase used to sum up the many ways in which the level of thinking can be developed in a classroom. However, the starting point is having something challenging and interesting to apply the thinking to!

Wings to fly

The phrase, 'Wings to fly, not drills to kill', comes from a wonderful evaluation we once heard about how a teacher employed more open and creative approaches to teaching and learning with her pupils. Risk-taking lies at the heart of any possibility for pupils to fly. They will do what we expect, so we should signify that writing in unusual ways is exciting. Of course, some will still need formats and templates as support resources.

Writing for reading

This has been a key feature of 'Opening Doors'. Teachers report that their pupils have a more confident approach to understanding a new text after writing on the same theme first.

Zoom closer

Using the language of media studies can be very useful. Just as a camera zooms in, so too can the teacher offer a magnified view of a particular image or concept by focusing on part of the text. A visualiser can quite literally 'zoom in' on the subject.

Bibliography

Primary sources

Adams, Richard (2014 [1972]). *Watership Down*. London: Oneworld Publications.

Adukwei-Bulley, Victoria (2017). 'How to Build a Kitchen', in *Rising Stars: New Young Voices in Poetry*. Hereford: Otter-Barry Books.

Alcott, Louisa May (1998 [1849]). *The Inheritance*. London: Penguin.

Alcott, Louisa May (2013 [1886]). *Jo's Boys*. N.p.: CreateSpace.

Alcott, Louisa May (2015 [1871]). *Little Men*. London: Puffin.

Alcott, Louisa May (2018 [1868]). *Little Women and Good Wives*. Ware: Wordsworth Classics.

Alexander, Kwame (2018). *Rebound*. London: Andersen Press.

Andersen, Hans Christian (1997 [1844]). *The Snow Queen*. Ware: Wordsworth Classics.

Angelou, Maya (1994a [1983]). 'Caged Bird', in *The Complete Collected Poems of Maya Angelou*. New York: Random House.

Angelou, Maya (1994b [1983]). 'Still I Rise', in *The Complete Collected Poems of Maya Angelou*. New York: Random House.

Atwood, Margaret (1996 [1970]). 'Woman Skating', in *Selected Poems 1965–1975*. Boston, MA: Houghton Mifflin.

Austen, Jane (2015 [1817]). *Northanger Abbey*. Ware: Wordsworth Classics.

Banyai, Istvan (1995). *Zoom*. London: Puffin Picture Books.

Banyai, Istvan (1998). *Re-Zoom*. London: Puffin Picture Books.

Bawden, Nina (2011 [1973]). *Carrie's War*. London: Puffin.

Bishop, Elizabeth (2011 [1946]). 'The Fish', in *Poems: The Centenary Edition*. London: Chatto & Windus.

Boyne, John (2006). *The Boy in the Striped Pyjamas*. London: David Fickling.

Bradbury, Ray (1993 [1950]). 'There Will Come Soft Rains', in Nicholas Fisk (ed.), *The Puffin Book of Science Fiction*. London: Puffin. Originally published in *The Martian Chronicles*.

Braithwaite, Eustace Edward Ricardo (2005 [1959]). *To Sir, With Love*. London: Vintage Classics.

Bramachari, Sita (2019). *Where the River Runs Gold*. London: Hodder and Stoughton.

Brontë, Anne (1997 [1846]). 'Lines Composed in a Wood on a Windy Day', in *The Brontës*. London: Everyman's Poetry.

Brontë, Charlotte (1921). 'Speak of the North!', in John Collings Squire (ed.), *A Book of Women's Verse*. Oxford: Clarendon Press. Available at: https://www.bartleby.com/291/118.html.

Brontë, Charlotte (1997 [1848]). 'Mementos', in *The Brontës*. London: Everyman's Poetry.

Brontë, Charlotte (2006 [1847]). *Jane Eyre*. London: Penguin.

Brontë, Emily (1995 [1847]). *Wuthering Heights*. Oxford: Oxford University Press.

Browning, Robert (1996 [1842]). 'The Pied Piper of Hamelin', in Robin Waterfield (ed.), *The Rime of the Ancient Mariner and Other Classic Stories in Verse*. London: Puffin Classics.

Brownlee, Liz (2018). 'Snow Fox', in Susannah Herbert (ed.), *Poetry for a Change: A National Poetry Day Anthology*. Hereford: Otter-Barry Books.

Causley, Charles (1992 [1966]). 'By St Thomas Water', in *Collected Poems 1951–2000*. London: Picador.

Causley, Charles (1992 [1988]). 'Eden Rock', in *Collected Poems, 1951–2000*. London: Picador.

Collins, Wilkie (1992 [1869]). *The Moonstone*. Ware: Wordsworth Classics.

Collins, Wilkie (1993 [1868]). *The Woman in White*. Ware: Wordsworth Classics.

Collins, Wilkie (2015 [1889]). *The Haunted Hotel*. London: Vintage Collins.

Conan Doyle, Arthur (1999 [1902]). 'The Hound of the Baskervilles', in *The Hound of the Baskervilles & The Valley of Fear*. Ware: Wordsworth Editions.

Cook, Abigail (2017). 'You Are the Ocean', in *Rising Stars: New Young Voices in Poetry*. Hereford: Otter-Barry Books.

Cook, Eliza (2018 [1840]). 'Song of Old Time', in Susannah Herbert (ed.), *Poetry for a Change: A National Poetry Day Anthology*. Hereford: Otter-Barry Books.

Cormier, Robert (2001 [1974]). *The Chocolate War*. London: Puffin.

Cornford, Frances (1987 [1948]). 'Childhood', in Fleur Adcock (ed.), *The Faber Book of 20th Century Women's Poetry*. London: Faber & Faber.

Cross, Gillian (2017 [1982]). *The Demon Headmaster*. Oxford: Oxford University Press.

Dahl, Roald (2013 [1988]). *Matilda*. London: Puffin.

Davies, Nicola (2017). *King of the Sky*, ill. Laura Carlin. London: Walker Books.

de la Mare, Walter (1941). 'The Snowflake', in *Bells and Grass*. London: Faber & Faber.

de la Mare, Walter (1979 [1938]). 'Brueghel's Winter', in *Collected Poems*. London: Faber & Faber.

Dharker, Imtiaz (2006). 'How to Cut a Pomegranate', in *The Terrorist at My Table*. Hexham: Bloodaxe Books.

Dickens, Charles (1992 [1849]). *David Copperfield*. Ware: Wordsworth Classics.

Dickens, Charles (1994 [1861]). *Great Expectations*. London: Penguin.

Dickens, Charles (1995 [1839]). *Nicholas Nickleby*. Ware: Wordsworth Classics.

Dickens, Charles (1996 [1857]). *Little Dorrit*. Ware: Wordsworth Classics.

Dickens, Charles (2000 [1837]). *Oliver Twist*. Ware: Wordsworth Classics.

Dickens, Charles (2016 [1866]). 'The Signalman', in *The Signalman: A Ghost Story for Christmas*. Windsor, ON: Biblioasis.

Dickens, Charles (2018 [1843]). *A Christmas Carol*. Ware: Wordsworth Classics.

Douglass, Frederick (2013 [1852]). 'What to the Slave is the Fourth of July?', in Shaun Usher (ed.), *Speeches of Note: A Celebration of the Old, New and Unspoken*. London: Hutchinson.

Duffy, Carol Ann (2004 [1993]). 'Valentine', in *New Selected Poems, 1984–2004*. London: Picador.

Duffy, Carol Ann (2007). 'The Alphabest', in *The Hat*. London: Faber & Faber.

du Maurier, Daphne (2003 [1938]). *Rebecca*. London: Virago.

Dunbar, Paul Laurence (2014 [1899]). 'Sympathy', in *Lyrics of the Hearthside*. Miami, FL: HardPress Publishing.

Edwards, Amelia B. (2010 [1864]). 'The Phantom Coach', in Vic Parker (ed.), *Classic Ghost Stories*. Thaxted: Miles Kelly.

Fleischman, Paul (2013). *The Matchbox Diary*. Somerville, MA: Candlewick Press.

Forward, Toby (2005). *The Wolf's Story: What Really Happened to Little Red Riding Hood*. London: Walker Books.

Frank, Anne (2007 [1947]). *The Diary of a Young Girl*. London: Puffin.

Frost, Robert (2001 [1922]). *Stopping by Woods on a Snowy Evening*. New York: Clearway.

Gaiman, Neil (2009). *The Graveyard Book*. London: Bloomsbury.

Gaiman, Neil (2013). *Coraline*. London: Bloomsbury.

Garfield, Leon (1973 [1969]). *Mr Corbett's Ghost*. Harmondsworth: Puffin.

Garlick, Raymond (2004). 'Alys at the Zoo', in *Fifty Strong: Fifty Poems Chosen by Teenagers for Teenagers*. Oxford: Heinemann.

Garner, Alan (1967 [2014]). *The Owl Service*. London: HarperCollins.

Gavin, Jamila (2000). *Coram Boy*. London: Mammoth.

Gleitzman, Morris (2009a). *Once*. London: Penguin.

Gleitzman, Morris (2009b). *Then*. London: Penguin.

Gray, Thomas (2015 [1751]). 'Elegy Written in a Country Churchyard', in *Selected Poems of Thomas Gray, Charles Churchill and William Cowper*. London: Penguin.

Greene, Graham (2004 [1938]). *Brighton Rock*. London: Vintage Classics.

Grill, William (2014). *Shackleton's Journey*. London: Flying Eye Books.

Gross, Philip (2018). *Dark Sky Park: Poems from the Edge of Nature*. Hereford: Otter-Barry Books.

Han-Shan (2013). *Cold Mountain Poems: Twenty-Four Poems by Han-Shan*, tr. Gary Snyder. Berkeley, CA: Counterpoint Press.

Hardy, Thomas (1974 [1912]). 'The Voice', in *Poems of Thomas Hardy*. London. Macmillan.

Harper, Frances (1866 [2013]). 'We Are All Bound Up Together', in Shaun Usher (ed.), *Speeches of Note: A Celebration of the Old, New and Unspoken*. London: Hutchinson.

Heron, E. and Heron, H. (2014 [1898]). 'The Story of Baelbrow', in *Ghosts: Being the Experiences of Flaxman Low*. London: Black Heath Editions.

Hill, Susan (1998 [1983]). *The Woman in Black*. London: Vintage.

Hilton, James (2015 [1933]). *Lost Horizon*. London: Vintage Classics.

Hines, Barry (2000 [1968]). *Kes*. London: Penguin.

Ho, Minfong (1991). *The Clay Marble*. Singapore: Marshall Cavendish.

Holub, Miroslav (1972). 'Fairy Tale', in Seamus Heaney and Ted Hughes (eds), *The Rattle Bag*. London: Faber & Faber.

Holub, Miroslav (1990 [1961]). 'Midday', in *Poems Before and After*. Hexham: Bloodaxe Books.

Holub, Miroslav (1990 [1963]). 'The New House', in *Poems Before and After*. Hexham: Bloodaxe Books.

Holub, Miroslav (2004 [1962]). 'The Door', in *Collected Later Poems 1988–2000*. Hexham: Bloodaxe Books.

Ho-Yen, Polly (2014). *Boy in the Tower*. London: Random House

Hughes, Langston (1994a [1924]). 'Being Old', in *The Collected Poems of Langston Hughes*. New York: Alfred. A. Knopf.

Hughes, Langston (1994b [1924]). 'I Dream a World', in *The Collected Poems of Langston Hughes*. New York: Alfred. A. Knopf.

Hughes, Langston (1994 [1926]). 'I, Too', in *The Collected Poems of Langston Hughes*. New York: Alfred A. Knopf.

Hughes, Langston (1994 [1925]). 'Mother to Son', in *The Collected Poems of Langston Hughes*. New York: Alfred A. Knopf.

Hughes, Ted (1995). 'The Thought Fox', in *New Selected Poems 1957–1994*. London: Faber & Faber.

Hughes, Ted (2015 [1957]). 'The Jaguar', in *The Hawk in the Rain*. London: Faber & Faber.

Ibbotson, Eva (2001). *Journey to the River Sea*. London: Macmillan.

James, Henry (2017 [1891]). *The Turn of the Screw and Other Stories*. London: Penguin.

James, Montague Rhodes (2007 [1895]). 'Lost Hearts', in *Collected Ghost Stories*. Ware: Wordsworth Classics.

James, Montague Rhodes (2007 [1904]). 'Number 13', in *Collected Ghost Stories*. Ware: Wordsworth Classics.

James, Montague Rhodes (2007 [1911]). 'The Tractate Middoth', in *Collected Ghost Stories*. Ware: Wordsworth Classics.

James, Montague Rhodes (2007 [1904]). 'The Treasure of Abbot Thomas', in *Collected Ghost Stories*. Ware: Wordsworth Classics.

Johnson, Georgia Douglas (2014 [1922]). 'When I Rise Up', in *Bronze: A Book of Verse*. Miami, FL: HardPress Publishing.

Johnson, James Weldon (2018a [1917]). 'The Gift to Sing', in *Fifty Years & Other Poems*. Boston, MA: Cornhill Company.

Johnson, James Weldon (2018b [1917]). 'To America', in *Fifty Years & Other Poems*. Boston, MA: Cornhill Company.

Kipling, Rudyard (1994 [1906]). 'Cities and Thrones and Powers', in *Collected Poems of Rudyard Kipling*. Ware: Wordsworth Classics.

Kipling, Rudyard (1994 [1910]). 'The Way Through the Woods', in *Collected Poems of Rudyard Kipling*. Ware: Wordsworth Classics.

Lear, Edward (1986 [1877]). *The Dong with a Luminous Nose*. New York: Lambda.

Lee, Laurie (2002 [1959]). *Cider with Rosie*. London: Vintage Classics.

Lessing, Doris (2002). 'Through the Tunnel', in *To Room Nineteen. Collected Stories: Volume 1*. Temecula, CA: Flamingo.

Lewis, Clive Staples (2009 [1950]). *The Lion, the Witch and the Wardrobe* (The Chronicles of Narnia). London: HarperCollins.

Lindsay, Joan (2013 [1967]). *Picnic at Hanging Rock*. London: Vintage Classics.

Litchfield, David (2015). *The Bear and the Piano*. London: Frances Lincoln Children's Books.

London, Jack (1977 [1908]). *That Spot*, in *Short Stories One*. Huddersfield: Schofield & Sims.

London, Jack (1992 [1903]). *Call of the Wild & White Fang*. Ware: Wordsworth Classics.

London, Jack (2008 [1902]). *To Build a Fire and Other Favourite Stories*. New York: Dover.

Lowbury, Edward (1990 [1972]). 'Prince Kano', in *Selected and New Poems, 1935–1989*. Frome: Hippopotamus.

Lowell, Amy (2015a [1912]). 'A Coloured Print by Shokei', in *A Dome of Many-Coloured Glass*. N.p.: CreateSpace.

Lowell, Amy (2015b [1912]). 'A Japanese Wood Carving', in *A Dome of Many-Coloured Glass*. N.p.: CreateSpace.

Lowell, Amy (2015c [1912]). 'The Pleiades', in *A Dome of Many-Coloured Glass*. N.p.: CreateSpace.

McCaughrean, Geraldine (2017). *Where the World Ends*. London: Usborne.

Machiavelli, Niccolò (1854). *The History of Florence and of the Affairs of Italy, from the Earliest Times to the Death of Lorenzo the Magnificent; Together with the Prince, and Various Historical Tracts*. London: Bohn.

MacKenzie, Ross (2015). *The Nowhere Emporium*. Edinburgh: Floris Books.

Magorian, Michelle (2014 [1981]). *Goodnight Mister Tom*. London: Puffin.

Mandela, Nelson (1994). *Long Walk to Freedom*. London: Little, Brown and Co.

Marvell, Andrew (2005 [1681]). 'To His Coy Mistress', in *The Complete Poems*. London: Penguin.

Melville, Herman (1992 [1851]). *Moby Dick*. Ware: Wordsworth Classics.

Messenger, Norman (2012). *The Land of Neverbelieve*. London: Walker Books.

Mew, Charlotte (1997 [1929]). 'The Call', in Val Warner (ed.), *Charlotte Mew: Collected Poems and Selected Prose*. Manchester: Fyfield Books.

Millwood-Hargrave, Kiran (2017). *The Island at the End of Everything*. Frome: Chicken House.

Morpurgo, Michael (2000). 'The Giant's Necklace', in *From Hereabout Hill*. London: Egmont.

Moses, Brian (2016). 'Ghosts of the London Underground', in *Lost Magic: The Very Best of Brian Moses*. London. Macmillan.

Naidoo, Beverley (2000). *The Other Side of Truth*. London: Random House.

Naidoo, Beverley (2008 [1985]). *Journey to Jo'Burg*. London: HarperCollins.

Nova, Karl (2017a). 'Lyrical Exercises', in *Rhythm and Poetry*. Steeton: Caboodle Books.

Nova, Karl (2017b). 'Underrated', in *Rhythm and Poetry*. Steeton: Caboodle Books.

Oswald, Alice (2012). 'A Star Here and a Star There', in Carol Ann Duffy (ed.), *101 Poems*. London: Macmillan.

Parker, Vic (ed.) (2010). *Classic Ghost Stories*. Thaxted: Miles Kelly.

Pepper, Dennis (ed.) (1994). *The Young Oxford Book of Ghost Stories*. Oxford: Oxford University Press.

Poe, Edgar Allan (1993 [1869]). 'The Fall of the House of Usher', in *Tales of Mystery and Imagination*. Ware: Wordsworth Editions.

Prevért, Jacques (2007). *How to Paint the Portrait of a Bird*, tr. Mordicai Gerstein. New York: Roaring Brook Press.

Pullman, Philip (1995). *Northern Lights* (His Dark Materials). London: Scholastic.

Ransome, Arthur (1916a). 'Daughter of the Snow', in *Old Peter's Russian Tales*. New York: Frederick A. Stokes.

Ransome, Arthur (1916b). 'Frost', in *Old Peter's Russian Tales*. New York: Frederick A. Stokes.

Reeves, James (2009 [1957]). 'The Snitterjipe', in *Complete Poems for Children*. London: Faber & Faber.

Rhys, Jean (1987 [1976]). 'I Used to Live Here Once', in *Collected Short Stories*. London: Penguin.

Riddell, Chris (2013). *Goth Girl and the Ghost of a Mouse*. London: Macmillan.

Rowling, Joanne K. (1997–2007). 'Harry Potter' Series. London: Bloomsbury.

Rowling, Joanne K. (2017). *Fantastic Beasts and Where to Find Them*, ill. Olivia Lomenech Gill. London: Bloomsbury Children's Books.

Rundell, Katherine (2015). *The Wolf Wilder*. London: Bloomsbury Children's Books.

Russell, Bertrand (2004 [1922]). 'Free Thought and Official Propaganda', in *Sceptical Essays*. Abingdon and New York: Routledge/Bertrand Russell Peace Foundation.

Sachar, Louis (2000). *Holes*. London: Bloomsbury.

Saint-Exupéry, Antoine de (2017 [1943]). *The Little Prince*, tr. Katherine Woods. London: Egmont Children's Books.

Scannell, Vernon (2001). 'Night Skating', in *The Very Best of Vernon Scannell*. London: Macmillan.

Scieszka, Jon (2012). *The True Story of the Three Little Pigs*. London: Puffin.

Scott, Robert Falcon (2005). *Captain Scott's Last Expedition*, ed. Max Jones. Oxford: Oxford University Press.

Seigel, Joshua (2018). 'The Both of Us', in Susannah Herbert (ed.), *Poetry for a Change: A National Poetry Day Anthology*. Hereford: Otter-Barry Books.

Sendak, Maurice (2000 [1963]). *Where the Wild Things Are*. London: Red Fox.

Shakespeare, William (2009 [1606]). 'Tomorrow, and Tomorrow, and Tomorrow' from *Macbeth*, in Michael Rosen (ed.), *Classic Poetry: An Illustrated Collection*. London: Walker Books.

Shelley, Mary (1992 [1823]). *Frankenstein*. Ware: Wordsworth Classics.

Shelley, Percy Bysshe (1994 [1818]). 'Ozymandias', in *The Selected Poetry and Prose of Shelley*. Ware: Wordsworth Poetry Library.

Shusterman, Neal (2007). *Unwind*. London: Simon & Schuster.

Smith, Dodie (2004 [1948]). *I Capture the Castle*. London: Vintage.

Spark, Muriel (2000 [1961]). *The Prime of Miss Jean Brodie*. London: Penguin.

Stafford, Fiona (ed.) (2013). *William Wordsworth and Samuel Taylor Coleridge: Lyrical Ballads, 1798 and 1802*. Oxford: Oxford University Press.

Stevenson, Robert Louis (1885). 'Escape at Bedtime', in *A Child's Garden of Verses*. Chicago, IL: M.A. Donohue and Co.

Stoker, Bram (1983 [1897]). *Dracula*. Oxford: Oxford University Press.

Summerfield, Geoffrey (ed.) (1970). *Voices: An Anthology of Poetry and Pictures*, 2 vols. (Harmondsworth: Penguin).

Swindells, Robert (2016 [1993]). *Stone Cold*. London: Penguin

Tan, Shaun (2000). *The Lost Thing*. London: Hodder Children's Books.

Tan, Shaun (2007). *The Arrival*. London: Hodder Children's Books.

Taylor, Mildred D. (1976). *Roll of Thunder, Hear My Cry*. London: Puffin.

Thomas, Dylan (2010 [1945]). 'Fern Hill', in *The Collected Poems of Dylan Thomas*. London: New Directions.

Thomas, Edward (1994 [1912]). 'The Path', in *The Works of Edward Thomas*. Ware: Wordsworth Poetry Library.

Uehashi, Nahoko (2006). *The Beast Player*. London: Pushkin Children's Books.

Van Allsburg, Chris (2011 [1984]). *The Mysteries of Harris Burdick*. London: Andersen Press.

Wakeling, Kate (2016). 'Spirit Bridge', in *Moon Juice: Poems for Children*. Birmingham: Emma Press.

Wells, Herbert George (2015 [1906]). 'The Door in the Wall', in *A Slip Under the Microscope*. London: Penguin.

Wells, Herbert George (2017 [1897]). *The Invisible Man & The Food of the Gods*. Ware: Wordsworth Classics.

Wiesner, David (2006). *Flotsam*. New York: Houghton Mifflin.

Williams, William Carlos (1973 [1935]). 'The Locust Tree in Flower', in Kenneth Koch, *Rose, Where Did You Get That Red? Teaching Great Poetry to Children*. New York. Vintage.

Williamson, Maurice (2018 [2013]). 'Be Ye Not Afraid', in Shaun Usher (ed.), *Speeches of Note: A Celebration of the Old, New and Unspoken*. London: Hutchinson.

Wordsworth, William (1994 [1807]). 'I Wandered Lonely as a Cloud', in *The Collected Poems of William Wordsworth*. Ware: Wordsworth Poetry Library.

Wynne Jones, Diana (2001). *The Time of the Ghost*. London: HarperCollins.

Yeats, William Butler (2000 [1888]). 'The Lake Isle of Innisfree', in *The Collected Poems of W. B. Yeats*. Ware: Wordsworth Editions.

Yeats, William Butler (2017 [1899]). 'The Song of Wandering Aengus', in *The Wind Among the Reeds*: London: Forgotten Books.

Yen Mah, Adeline (1999). *Chinese Cinderella: The True Story of an Unwanted Daughter*. Harlow: Pearson.

Yousafzai, Malala (2013). *I Am Malala: The Girl Who Stood Up for Education and Was Shot by the Taliban*. London: Weidenfeld & Nicolson.

Secondary sources

Bandura, Albert (1997). *Self-efficacy: The Exercise of Control*. New York: Freeman.

Bandura, Albert (2006). 'Adolescent Development from an Agentic Perspective', in Frank Pajares and Tim Urdan (eds), *Self-Efficacy Beliefs of Adolescents*. Charlotte, NC: Information Age Publishing, pp. 1–35.

Bleiman, Barbara (2018). 'Overemphasising the Vocabulary Challenge?', *English & Media Centre* (21 March). Available at: https://www.englishandmedia.co.uk/blog/overemphasising-the-vocabulary-challenge.

Bruner, Jerome (1983). *Child's Talk: Learning to Use Language*. New York: Norton.

Clarke, Shirley (2014). *Outstanding Formative Assessment: Culture and Practice*. London: Hodder Education.

Cox, Bob (2014). *Opening Doors to Famous Poetry and Prose: Ideas and Resources for Accessing Literary Heritage Works*. Carmarthen: Crown House Publishing.

Cox, Bob (2016a). *Opening Doors to Quality Writing: Ideas for Writing Inspired by Great Writers for Ages 6 to 9*. Carmarthen: Crown House Publishing.

Cox, Bob (2016b). *Opening Doors to Quality Writing: Ideas for Writing Inspired by Great Writers for Ages 10 to 13*. Carmarthen: Crown House Publishing.

Eagleton, Ian (2019). 'The Beauty, Drama and Mischief of Poetry: An Interview with Kate Wakeling', *The Reading Realm* (6 March). Available at: https://thereadingrealm.co.uk/2019/03/06/the-beauty-drama-and-mischief-of-poetry-an-interview-with-kate-wakeling/.

Eyre, Deborah (2016). *High Performance Learning: How to Become a World Class School*. Abingdon and New York: Routledge.

Hattie, John (2012). *Visible Learning for Teachers: Maximizing Impact on Learning*. Abingdon and New York: Routledge.

Hirsch Jr, Eric Donald (2003). 'Reading Comprehension Requires Knowledge', *American Educator* (spring). Available at: https://www.aft.org/sites/default/files/periodicals/Hirsch.pdf.

Koch, Kenneth (1973). *Rose, Where Did You Get That Red? Teaching Great Poetry to Children*. New York: Random House.

Kosmoski, Georgia, Gay, Geneva and Vockell, Edward (1990). 'Cultural Literacy and Academic Achievement', *Journal of Experimental Education*, 58(4): 265–272.

Lemov, Doug, Driggs, Colleen and Woolway, Erica (2016). *Reading Reconsidered: A Practical Guide to Rigorous Literacy Instruction*. San Francisco, CA: Jossey-Bass.

Meek, Margaret (1988). *How Texts Teach What Readers Learn*. Stroud: Thimble Press.

Myatt, Mary (2018). *The Curriculum: Gallimaufry to Coherence*. Woodbridge: John Catt Educational.

Quigley, Alex (2018). *Closing the Vocabulary Gap*. Abingdon and New York: Routledge.

Quigley, Alex, Muijs, Daniel and Stringer, Eleanor (2019). *Metacognition and Self-Regulated Learning: Guidance Report*. London: Education Endowment Foundation. Available at: https://educationendowmentfoundation.org.uk/evidence-summaries/teaching-learning-toolkit/meta-cognition-and-self-regulation/.

Rosen, Michael (2016). *What is Poetry? The Essential Guide to Reading and Writing Poems*. London: Walker Books.

Shanahan, Timothy (2017). 'The Instructional Level Concept Revisited: Teaching with Complex Text', *Shanahan on Literacy* [blog] (7 February). Available at: https://shanahanonliteracy.com/blog/the-instructional-level-concept-revisited-teaching-with-complex-text.

Stephen, Martin and Warwick, Ian (2015). *Educating the More Able Student: What Works and Why*. London: SAGE.

Tennent, Wayne (2015). *Understanding Reading Comprehension: Processes and Practices*. London: Sage Publications Ltd.

Tennent, Wayne, Reedy, David, Gamble, Nikki and Hobsbaum, Angela (2016). *Guiding Readers – Layers of Meaning: A Handbook for Teaching Reading Comprehension to 7–11 Year Olds*. London: University College London Institute of Education Press.

Warwick, Ian and Speakman, Ray (2018). *Redefining English for the More Able: A Practical Guide*. Abingdon and New York: Routledge.

Waugh, Steven (2001). *Essential Modern World History*. Oxford: Oxford University Press.

Willingham, Daniel (2006). 'How Knowledge Helps', *American Educator* (spring). Available at: https://www.aft.org/periodical/american-educator/spring-2006/how-knowledge-helps.

Willingham, Daniel (2017). *The Reading Mind: A Cognitive Approach to Understanding How the Mind Reads*. San Francisco, CA: Jossey-Bass.

Useful websites

American Federation of Teachers: www.aft.org

Book Trust: www.booktrust.org.uk

Centre for Literacy in Primary Education: www.clpe.org.uk

Changing Minds (Socratic questions): http://changingminds.org/techniques/questioning/socratic_questions.htm

Education Endowment Foundation: https://educationendowmentfoundation.org.uk

English and Media Centre: www.englishandmedia.co.uk

English Association (4–11 online articles): www2.le.ac.uk/offices/english-

association/primary/primary-plus/
411online

High Performance Learning: www.
highperformancelearning.co.uk

Into Film: www.intofilm.org

Just Imagine Story Centre: www.
justimagine.co.uk

Let's Think in English: www.
letsthinkinenglish.org

Michael Rosen: www.michaelrosen.co.uk

More Able and Talented (Wales): http://
matwales.org

National Association for the Teaching of
English: www.nate.org.uk

National Literacy Trust: www.literacytrust.
org.uk

National Poetry Day: www.
nationalpoetryday.co.uk

Poetry Archive: www.poetryarchive.org

Poetry by Heart: www.poetrybyheart.
org.uk

Poetry Society: www.poetrysociety.org.uk

Potential Plus UK: www.potentialplusuk.
org

Society for the Advancement of
Philosophical Enquiry and Reflection in
Education: www.sapere.org.uk

SOLO taxonomy: www.johnbiggs.com.
au/academic/solo-taxonomy

Talk for Writing: www.talk4writing.co.uk

United Kingdom Literacy Association:
https://ukla.org

List of Downloadable Resources

Available from: https://crownhouse.co.uk/ featured/opening-doors-richer-10-13

About the Authors

Bob Cox

Having taught English for twenty-three years, Bob Cox is now an independent education consultant, writer and teacher coach who works nationally and internationally to support outstanding learning. Bob also delivers keynotes for national associations, multi-academy trusts and local authorities, as more schools integrate 'Opening Doors' strategies into their curriculum design.

Leah Crawford

Leah Crawford has fifteen years' experience as a local authority English inspector and adviser, working across both the primary and secondary phases, and now leads the Thinktalk education consultancy. She is an associate tutor on King's College London's Let's Think in English cognitive acceleration programme and also works in support of a European Erasmus project on the assessment of thinking skills.

Verity Jones

Having spent over a decade working in education – as a teacher, a deputy head and an adviser – Verity Jones is now a senior lecturer at the University of the West of England, Bristol. She continues to provide training for both new and experienced teachers on how to ensure every child reaches their potential.

Support:
List all the objects inside the boat, including the bedroom. Can you suggest links or connections?

Support:
How is the description of the bedroom linked with David's emotions?
How important is the description of the food?

How does Dickens use descriptive language to support meaning and themes?

Support:
Can you write about the overall atmosphere of the main room?
How does the way David sees the objects link with the nature of the Peggotty family? Are they 'rough and ready'?
Why is the way David approaches the boat significant?

Greater depth:
Explore in detail all the ways in which Dickens builds the charm of the home and how David's confidence grows. Is Dickens saying anything about poverty?
Compare and contrast the methods with other passages from Dickens and other sections from *David Copperfield* featuring Mr Murdstone.

❦ Show how David's emotions are linked to what he sees, and why.

Key concept: setting and theme – visualising a specific scene via detailed description

❦ Use increasingly complex examples to show how an overall impression mounts of the scene in the boat.

❦ Include David's response to people and the links between setting and theme.

There are many opportunities for **dialogic talk** and **didactic teaching**, too, to ensure that the children's love and appreciation of this famous episode is cemented. Try preparing your teaching priorities around the following themes:

❦ The sea.

❦ The nature of the home.

❦ Poverty and love.

❦ The romance and charm of the setting through David's eyes – is the smell of fish charming to the reader?

❦ The more distinctive emotions expressed in the bedroom theme.

❦ The way David sees the members of the Peggotty family.

❦ Food! See the food description in *Great Expectations* at Joe Gargery's house (Chapter 4) for comparison.

❦ The repeated linking of objects to meaning and narrative technique.

Beyond the limit – link reading

These texts should enable your pupils to read examples of writers zooming closer to give readers in-depth descriptions but often with a narrator who has a particular mood on how he or she sees it (as in Wallace's description of the garden in Unit 10). Some of them also reflect characters who are searching for a home or an identity.

- *The Phantom Coach* by Amelia Edwards (Unit 2 in *Opening Doors to Quality Writing for Ages 10 to 13*)
- *The Matchbox Diary* by Paul Fleischman
- *Mr Corbett's Ghost* by Leon Garfield
- *Brighton Rock* by Graham Greene (the description at the start of Bank Holiday crowds)
- *The Clay Marble* by Minfong Ho
- *Journey to the River Sea* by Eva Ibbotson (e.g. Chapter 2 – the journey down the Amazon)
- 'Through the Tunnel' by Doris Lessing
- *Where the World Ends* by Geraldine McCaughrean
- *The Nowhere Emporium* by Ross MacKenzie
- *The Other Side of Truth* and *Journey to Jo'burg* by Beverley Naidoo
- 'I Used to Live Here Once' by Jean Rhys
- *The Little Prince* by Antoine de Saint-Exupéry
- *The Lost Thing* by Shaun Tan
- *Chinese Cinderella* by Adeline Yen Mah

Other books by Charles Dickens:

- *A Christmas Carol*
- *David Copperfield*
- *Great Expectations* (Unit 8 in *Opening Doors to Famous Poetry and Prose*)
- *Little Dorrit*

Wings to fly

The **zoom closer** strategy can be added to the many and varied ways in which your pupils start to comprehend challenging texts. The more styles of writing they can add to their repertoire, the more confident they will become when faced with unseen texts:

> When readers engage with texts, they bring to bear their unique life experiences including their own reading histories. Thus, the sense readers make of a text is more likely to be unique … For this reason, telling readers what to comprehend is of limited value. It is more helpful to give them access to tools that will show them *how* to comprehend. (Tennent et al., 2016: 44)

Bob says …

The whole process of reading literature can be signposted as a lifelong journey of enquiry – a much richer curriculum goal than reading narrowly for test practice.